D0264746

Other Hamlyn titles in this series you will enjoy:
The Hamlyn Book of Ghosts   ISBN 0 600 34053 8
The Hamlyn Book of Horror   ISBN 0 600 34558 0

The Hamlyn Book of
Mysteries

Bernard Brett

HAMLYN
London · New York · Sydney · Toronto

Acknowledgements

Academy of Applied Science, Massachusetts 137 bottom left; Columbia Pictures Industries, Inc. 2-3; Claudia Andujar 38; BBC Hulton Picture Library, London 103; British Museum, London 90; British Tourist Authority, London 117; Central Press, London 26; John H. Cutten, London 115; René Dahinden/Fortean Picture Library 65 top, 65 centre, 65 bottom; Deutsche Fotothek Dresden 92; Mary Evans Picture Library, London 16, 17, 23 inset, 44, 48, 51, 85 top, 94, 97, 123, 124, 150; Fortean Picture Library, Montgomery 6-7, 20, 21 left, 21 right, 46, 67 top right, 67 bottom left, 67 bottom right, 81, 137 top, 137 bottom right, 154-155; Rick Frehsee, Miami 152-153, 153; Photographie Giraudon, Paris 88; Hamlyn Group-Kershaw Studios, York 128, 129, 129 inset; Hamlyn Group Picture Library 86, 140, 144 top, 144 bottom; Michael Herridge, London 8-9; Lord Hunt 60; Jeffrey Iverson, Cardiff 119; Kobal Collection, London 107; Kungl. biblioteket, Stockholm 96; Donald Macinnes, Stornoway 10, 12, 13; Mansell Collection, London 71, 72, 75, 83, 105, 147; Mansell Collection-BBC 135; Mas, Barcelona 84, 85 bottom; Museum of London 149; National Portrait Gallery, London 55 top, 55 bottom, 121; Popperfoto, London 15, 18, 25, 26-27, 28, 29, 30-31, 59 top, 95, 106 top, 106 bottom, 148; Psychic News, London 37; Royal Geographical Society, London 58, 59 bottom, 64, 67 top left, 93; Syndication International, London 134; Twentieth Century Fox 22-23; US Navy, Washington, D.C. 110-111, 113, 114.

The extract which appears on page 62 is taken from *Ascent of Everest* by John Hunt, published by Hodder & Stoughton Ltd. It is reprinted here by permission of Hodder & Stoughton Ltd.

The story 'Have we lived before' which appears on pages 116-128 is based on the book *More Lives Than One* by J Iverson, published by Souvenir Press Ltd.

Illustrated by:
Harry Bishop, Mike Codd, Brian Denington, Peter Dennis, Bill Donohoe, Oliver Frey, Ivan Lapper, John Raynes, Dave Williams, Paul Wright

Cover illustration
Oliver Frey

First published 1983 by The Hamlyn Publishing Group Limited
London · New York · Sydney · Toronto
Astronaut House, Feltham, Middlesex, England

© Copyright The Hamlyn Publishing Group Limited 1983
All rights reserved. No part of this publication may be reproduced, stored in a retrieval system, or transmitted, in any form or by any means, electronic, mechanical, photocopying, recording or otherwise, without the permission of The Hamlyn Publishing Group Limited and the copyright holder.

ISBN 0 600 36420 8
Printed in Italy

Contents

Introduction

Everybody loves a mystery . . . From the very beginning, people have been both frustrated and intrigued by mysterious happenings that would seem to have no rational explanation. They have sought to ferret out the truth, tie up loose ends and round off the story with a nice neat answer. Some people have spent a lifetime delving into their favourite mystery, often producing an explanation which, with hindsight, appears painfully obvious and logical. Others have exposed frauds such as the 'Piltdown Man', a supposedly early form of man that was thought to have existed when some bones were found in Piltdown, Sussex, England, in 1912. The collection of bones was, much later, discovered to be a hoax.

Yet, some mysteries remain unsolved. What did happen aboard the *Mary Celeste*? Did the Devil really stalk across Devon during a snowy night in 1855? Something did leave a track in Devon one night. The weight of evidence supplied by eye-witnesses is too convincing to be dismissed out of hand. Does a mysterious force lurk in the 'Bermuda Triangle' or, dare I say it, are the disappearances the work of creatures from out of space?

Perhaps in time these mysteries will give up their secrets one by one. But until then they remain unexplained.

The Eilean Mor Light

Above him towered the lighthouse. There was still no sign of life and he sensed that something was very wrong.

As the hump of Eilean Mor loomed out of the grey December day, Joseph Moore could just make out the shape of the lighthouse perched at the top. Eilean Mor is the most northern of the seven Flannan Isles, known as the Seven Hunters. They are desolate piles of rock jutting out into the Atlantic Ocean, 25 kilometres west of Lewis, in the Hebrides, Scotland. The Flannans are all similar in appearance, none of them measures much more than 450 by 180 kilometres. Their dark cliffs rise a sheer 60 metres out of the water and are crowned with sparse stretches of turf. No one lives there, although tradition has it that the ruined chapel on Eilean Mor was built by St Flannan, the hermit Bishop of Killaloe. The Seven Hunters have an evil reputation with seafaring folk; many a proud vessel has been dashed to pieces on the jagged rocks at the base of the cliffs. They have always been a menace to shipping in fog and in the fierce gales that hit this area.

Trinity House (a corporation which deals with lighthouses, lightships and buoys around the shores of Britain) started building a lighthouse on Eilean Mor in 1895. It was no easy task. A landing had to be hewn out of solid rock and a zig-zag flight of steps cut into the 60-metre cliffs on both sides of the islet, so that some protection could be offered, whatever the direction of the prevailing wind. It took four years to complete, but finally, in 1899 its light shone out, 85 metres above the sea.

It was a lonely spot and four keepers were assigned to the Eilean Mor light. There were always three on duty and one ashore. In theory each man did six weeks duty then had two weeks leave, but winter gales played havoc with this routine. Such was the case in 1900 when Assistant keeper, Joseph Moore, should have been landed on 20 December, but heavy seas had prevented a boat-landing until Boxing Day. Not a day to commence a turn of duty, but at least he had had Christmas Day at home.

Smoke streaming from her stack, the tender, *Hesperus,* butted her way through the Atlantic rollers. Within the hour they would be under the shelter of the eastern cliffs, landing the

These ruins on the island could be evidence of a freak wave.

10

relief keeper, stores and the belated Christmas presents. After a six week turn of duty it was a great occasion when the tender arrived, and the on-duty keepers always hurried down to the landing to wave her in, eager for news from the mainland. Joe, standing next to the skipper on the bridge, turned his glasses on to the rock. No sign of life yet, but surely *Hesperus* must have been spotted. Everything looked calm and peaceful, and there was no evidence of any damage caused by the recent storms.

Hesperus lay wallowing in the swell beneath the cliffs. She gave a blast on her whistle, a boat was lowered and the crew climbed aboard. Soon they were pulling for the nearby jetty but there was still no sign of the on-duty keepers.

Joe jumped ashore and began the steep climb to the summit, while the boat's crew began landing the stores. Towards the top Joe paused for breath. Above him towered the lighthouse. There was still no sign of life and he sensed that something was very wrong. But what could it be? It was unlike Jim Ducat, the head keeper, and the two assistant keepers, Tom Marshall and Donald McArthur not to come to meet him. Usually the man to be relieved stood waiting, bag packed, on the landing, eager to get ashore. Then Joe glanced up at the lantern tower. To his surprise, the daytime cloth was not covering the lens. It was a strict Trinity House regulation that this should be done without fail every morning. Not once, during the year that the lighthouse had been open, had the keepers failed to do this before. Something was definitely wrong.

Everything was quiet, except for the sound of the waves beating on the rocks far below and the screams of the seabirds circling the cliffs. Hurrying up the remaining steps, Joe made for the lighthouse door which was shut but unlocked. Nervously opening it, he stepped inside – dead silence.

'Hello. Anybody about?' His voice echoed through the circular rooms – no reply. Could they all have been taken ill at the same time? He dashed up the stairs to the living quarters – empty. Up and up he ran to the lantern room – no one there. The lighthouse was empty. Panic-stricken he ran out and down the cliff steps. The men unloading the stores stared at him in amazement. They listened in disbelief as he stammered out his story. How could three men just disappear? Surely they would not attempt to reach the mainland with a gale blowing, whatever the reason. Anyway their boat was still in its cradle.

Two of the crew went back with Joe to make a thorough inspection, while the others rowed back to *Hesperus* to report to the skipper. They started on the lower store room, and floor by floor they searched all over the lighthouse and then the tiny island. There was no doubt about it, the three keepers had vanished. In the lantern room the light had been extinguished, the wicks had been trimmed, the oil fountains had been filled up and the lenses had been polished, which suggested that the keepers had left after completing the morning chores.

Nowadays, the Eilean Mor lighthouse, scene of the disaster, is automatically controlled.

12

Two recent keepers of the lighthouse.

The mystery deepened. Two sets of oilskins and sea boots were missing, those of Ducat and Marshall. McArthur's coat was still hanging up, his sea boots standing neatly beneath it. He must have been inside when something had happened which had sent him scurrying out of the lighthouse without waiting to put on his oilskin and boots. Whatever it was, had happened on 15 December, as the last entry that there was in the head keeper's log was headed 09.00 hours on that day in 1900. According to the log, a westerly gale blowing on the 12 and 13 December had dropped to a stiff breeze by the 14 December, so the following day must have been comparatively calm. Anyway, no keeper in his right mind would venture out during a fierce gale.

And it had been a fierce gale. When Joe Moore and his companions examined the steps and landing on the west side, they found the iron railings along the edge of the steps twisted and dislodged in places. More than halfway down the steps was a concrete platform on which a crane was mounted. This was undamaged and the jib secured, but a heavy box, stowed in a crevice 12 metres above, had been washed away and torn open, its ropes and tackle scattered about the cliff face. A concrete block weighing about a tonne had been displaced and swept some distance away. The waves piling against the side of the cliff must have reached the incredible height of 33 metres to do this damage. However, there was no clue to the whereabouts of the keepers.

One possible explanation was later put forward to explain the mystery. It was discovered some time after, that on occasions the sea, probably influenced by a freak tide, would lift over the west landing. One moment it would be calm, the next a high wave would surge across the landing. Anyone standing there would be washed away and drowned. This curious phenomenon had never happened during the first year that the lighthouse was in operation, but several times since, unwary keepers have had narrow escapes.

Had Ducat and Marshall been swept away while inspecting the storm damage? Did McArthur, see it happen from the lantern room, rush down, to try to save them, and get swept away himself? Or is there a more sinister explanation?

13

Unidentified Flying Objects

The UFO came spinning at them out of the sky, shot above the car, then stopped and returned, making two or three more passes over the car before it flew off.

A young man, Norman Muscarello, looked at his watch – 2.00 am. He had been visiting a friend in Amesbury, Massachusetts, USA, and not having a car of his own, he had set out on foot to cover the 19 kilometres to Exeter, New Hampshire, hoping to hitch a lift. However, the traffic was light on Route 150 and he had walked most of the way. Cold, tired and dispirited, he tramped on; there were still a few kilometres to go.

He was not a nervous man, but it was pitch black on this part of Route 150, with open fields either side, and once or twice he glanced apprehensively over his shoulder. Then he saw it. Coming directly towards him across an open field was what appeared to be a huge round shape as big as a house, travelling not much more than a metre above the ground. He later estimated that it was about 25 metres in diameter and said that a row of bright, pulsating lights cast a red glow around the centre. The weird craft seemed to wobble in the air as it rushed silently towards him. In a panic he threw himself into a nearby ditch, but he watched the 'thing' as he later described it, move away, its rim of winking lights vanishing into the distance.

Recovering his wits, he scrambled out of the ditch to the nearest house. Shouting and calling, he hammered on the door with his fists, but there was no answer. The place was empty. Unsure what to do next, he looked around. The 'thing' had disappeared but it was a long way to the next house. Headlights in the distance helped him to decide. He ran into the highway madly waving his arms and the car slowed down. A surprised middle-aged couple could see that he was badly shaken and agreed to take him to the police station in Exeter.

At the station he began to babble out his story to the desk officer. He was still badly frightened and not making much sense. Good-naturedly the policeman listened to what he had to say. An object as big as a house floating through the air sounded like a hoax, but the lad was obviously upset and seemed sincere enough. Reluctantly he called in a patrol car over the radio. He could guess what Eugene Bertrand, the patrolman, would have to say when he heard the story. But the patrolman had a strange report of his own to make when he arrived. He had pulled off the highway to investigate a parked car and found the driver shaking with fright. She had said that a large airborne object with flashing red lights had followed her car. Desperately she had managed to keep ahead of it, but when it had disappeared she had drawn off the road and collapsed over the wheel. At the time Bertrand had believed that the woman had imagined it all, but after listening to Norman's story later he began to wonder.

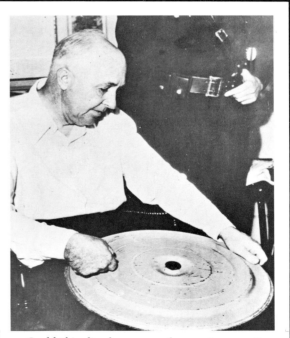

Could this disc have come from outer space? Russell Long, seen here holding it, believes it may have done. One day in July, 1947, it mysteriously appeared in the garden of his north Hollywood home in California. Falling from an apparently empty sky, it landed in a flowerbed and skidded into a wall.

15

This photograph of swiftly moving lights was taken at Salem Air Base, Massachusetts. Some people believe they are just light reflections.

The two policemen looked at each other. This was something beyond their experience and there was nothing in the police manual about how to deal with flying objects the size of houses. It would be wise to move cautiously.

'Better take the lad back, Eugene, and have a look.'

It was getting on for 3.00 am when Norman and officer Bertrand arrived at the field where Norman had seen the 'thing'. From the highway everything appeared quiet and still. The patrolman climbed out of the car, and leading the way with a powerful torch, he began to walk into the field with Norman behind him. 'Sure it wasn't a helicopter, Son?'

Norman was about to answer, when there it was again. 'I see it. I see it,' he shouted.

Bertrand swung round in time to see a large round object rise slowly from behind the trees and move silently towards them. Grabbing the gaping Norman, the officer ran with him to the parked patrol car, jumped in, slammed the door and shouted into the microphone, 'I've seen it myself'. For several minutes the flying object hovered about 30 metres above the ground, in absolute silence. Fearfully, the two men watched it as it began to move off gathering speed. They had no difficulty in making out its shape as the whole countryside around it was bathed in a red glow. Another patrol car screeched to a halt alongside them. Patrolman David Hunt could hardly believe his eyes. The mysterious craft was now moving in the direction of the Atlantic Ocean.

A mysterious line of unidentified aircraft that was photographed over Montreal, Canada, in August 1973.

The three men agreed on what they had seen and back at the police station they made a joint report. They described the lights, five of them in a row, as being bright red and the size of base balls. Tilted at an angle of 60°, they flashed in sequence along the row and back again. Could it be something to do with the nearby Air Force base? If it was an aircraft it was certainly not one that they had ever seen before, and was the Air Force likely to be testing a new model at night, flying so low in the vicinity of towns?

White as a ghost, Norman was delivered to his anxious mother, who found it difficult to believe her son's story, until the investigating officers came to question him next day. The two Air Force officers were used to this sort of thing. They were trained to sift fact from fantasy, and to them this was just another UFO (Unidentified Flying Object) investigation. This one lasted several days, during which time they discovered that there had been simultaneous sightings throughout the area. As the news spread other people came forward, many of them reluctantly, to claim sightings, and saucer-watching became a popular pastime.

Norman was about to join the Navy, but he decided that he would try to see the 'thing' again before reporting to the Naval Training

He was taking a picture of a Vulcan bomber. But a mysterious shape turned up on the film

WHAT WAS THIS PUZZLE IN THE SKY?

I T is six o'clock on the evening of December 12 last. A Vulcan bomber, ready for action, stands on the tarmac at Coningsby R.A.F. station, Lincolnshire. *TV Times* photographer Peter Bolton focuses his camera and takes several shots.

The result you can see on the right. A bomber in close-up—and above it, a strange object of perfect aerodynamic shape.

What is it? Photographer Bolton doesn't know. He didn't see it through his view-finder. He has checked his camera and film. All were in order.

It looks, of course, like a flying saucer. But that sounds such a ridiculous explanation.

Does it? Two R.A.F. boy entrants at Cosford Training Establishment, Shropshire, claim that they saw a similar object actually land five days before Bolton took his picture.

It came down, and disappeared behind a hangar. A green beam shone from it, sweeping around like a searchlight. They watched it for two minutes, then went to tell the duty officer. But when they returned, it had gone.

The chaplain at Cosford said later: "The boys believe they saw a trap door in the upper part open slowly. They are sane, sensible lads."

And on September 16, 1963, Michael Blake, a Southampton schoolboy, saw an unidentified object travelling towards the coast. Later he sketched what he saw.

And the result is remarkably like that strange shape hovering over the Vulcan. . . .

GEORGE BRUCE

The Vulcan bomber and (enlarged, on the left) the mystery object. The schoolboy sketch (right) bears an uncanny likeness. Is it coincidence?

Very bright 'halo' (Like a kind of mist)

Silvery metallic body "Highly polished"

A camera fault, an atmospheric disturbance, or are we being watched?

Centre. Night after night he and a group of friends watched in the fields off Route 150 where he had first seen his UFO. They had no luck. Then someone suggested an all-night vigil. To the chattering young folk it was all very much a game, although it began to pall during the early hours of the morning. Just as the sun was rising, Norman spotted his second UFO. Saucer-shaped and blue-metallic in colour it floated across the clear dawn sky.

Then the sifting began. The two investigating officers logged each reported sighting and assessed its value as evidence. It was a warm, clear night as Ron Smith was driving near Exeter with his mother and aunt. The UFO came spinning at them out of the sky, shot above the car, then stopped and returned, making two or three more passes over the car before it flew off. Ron carried on to Exeter, but then, although badly frightened, they decided to go back for another look. The UFO, seemingly back on patrol, dived at them once and then disappeared for good. In their report, Ron Smith and his passengers described the aircraft as a large, oval-shaped object with a bright red light near the top, and a glowing white light beneath its body.

Another Exeter woman claimed that she had seen a large, red blinking light in the sky one night. It moved in her direction, stopped, then veered off again in another direction. She could not see its shape clearly, but thought it might have been conical. Under close questioning she continued to maintain that it could not have been a conventional aircraft as no aeroplane could stop in midair, then shoot off again.

At the same time there were a number of daylight sightings in the Exeter area. One UFO was reported as a wingless, metal-coloured object, able to reverse direction and make abrupt changes of speed. As sighting followed sighting from the same area, the press began to take an interest at a national level, and a journalist, John Fuller, started an investigation prior to writing an article.

It came to light that at least 60 people believed they had seen a UFO in the Exeter area; many more were reluctant to come forward. Some of these witnesses were obviously unreliable, others very reliable. A few had a story that was difficult to account for. Two

The friends watched all night in the fields.

experienced police officers and a young man seeing the same thing at the same time constituted good evidence. By the time Fuller had finished his interviewing, he was no longer sceptical, and he concluded that the most likely answer to the sightings was that Exeter had received a visit from interplanetary space ships.

The Air Force, in its report issued on 27 October 1965, refused to accept this explanation. Apparently there had been a high-altitude exercise called 'Big Beast' in the Exeter area on the night that Norman Muscarello had been walking home and they suggested that the UFO seen by him and Officers Bertrand and Hunt could well have been B.47 jets. They also suggested that the men might have been confused by stars and planets twinkling more than they normally did, and moving in unusual formations. To most people in Exeter this sounded a bit thin. Could so many of them have been misled, and what about the daylight sightings?

19

Kenneth Arnold, who saw some flying saucers.

UFO – Unidentified Flying Object!

It all started, or rather what is sometimes called the modern age of flying saucers started, during the Second World War, when British and American pilots began reporting strange balls of fire seen during high-altitude missions over Germany. It was 1944. These 'Kraut fireballs' or 'foo-fighters' either flew alongside the aircraft or followed them at a distance, often in formations of up to 20. No matter how the pilots tried, they were unable to shake off their unwanted escorts. The balls of fire were also seen later by American pilots over Japan. Could these glowing balls that changed from red to orange to white and back again to red, be a German-Japanese secret weapon? If so why didn't they attack? After the war there came the disturbing news that German pilots had experienced the same 'foo-fighters', in their turn believing them to be a secret weapon of the Allies. Although interesting, the reports were not taken too seriously except by the pilots who had seen them.

Then in June 1947, there was a sudden quickening of interest. Kenneth Arnold, a 32-year-old salesman, was flying a private plane from Chehalis to Yakima in the United States. He had never heard of UFOs or flying saucers; they meant nothing to him. However, he was keeping a sharp look out for a military transport plane that had disappeared in the area. As he flew over the Cascade Range of mountains in the State of Washington, he searched the ground for any reflection of sunlight from the wings or fuselage of a crashed aircraft. At about 3.00 pm he noticed a flash of light in the sky off his port wing. To his amazement this proved to be a formation of nine unfamiliar aircraft. 'I could see their outlines quite plainly against the snow as they approached the mountain.' He reported later:

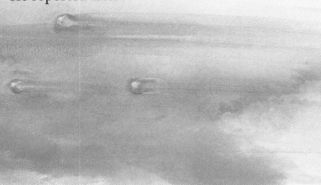

'They flew very close to the mountain tops, directly south east down the hog's back of the range, flying like geese in a diagonal chain-like line, as if they were linked together.'

As he watched, the strange craft dipped and changed course two at a time. 'They were approximately 20 or 25 miles [30 to 40 kilometres] away,' Arnold went on:

'and I couldn't see a tail on them. I watched for about three minutes . . . a chain of saucer-like things at least 5 miles [8 kilometres] long, swerving in and out of the high mountain peaks. They were flat like a pie pan and so shiny they reflected the sun like a mirror.'

He calculated that they were travelling at something like 2730 kph. At that time it was three times faster than any known aircraft.

His report created a sensation. Newspapers and magazines throughout the world carried the story. The strange aircraft, christened Flying Saucers by the press were talked about from London to Tokyo. Old, even ancient reports, which until then had been dismissed as fiction, hysteria or folk legends, were viewed in a different light. Had there been visitations from outer space before? The Egyptians and Mesopotamians spoke of fiery chariots in the sky. The Romans reported ships sailing across the heavens, globes and a burning shield which crossed the sky from west to east.

These 16th-century woodcuts represent 'a very frightful spectacle' seen over Nuremburg in 1561 (left), and large black globes that appeared in the sky at Basle (right). They may look far-fetched, but they were made in all good faith.

During the Middle Ages the accounts became more detailed, but even. more far-fetched. A 13th century Frenchman wrote of a large bright star which rose in the sky, travelled north, then suddenly disappeared. An observer in England, in 1323, Robert of Reading, reported a fiery shape the size of a small boat that crossed the sky from south to north. It was noticed from the ground that when a bright red flame burst from the front of the object its speed increased dramatically. Countless reports appear in the chronicles of the time, all very similar. In the 17th century, some formations of flying ships were seen by Spanish sailors, and John Evelyn, an English diarist, claimed to have seen:

'a shining cloud in the air, in shape resembling a sword, point reaching to the north. It was as bright as the moon, the rest of the sky [at night] being serene. It began about eleven at night and vanished not till about one, being seen by all the south of England.'

One evening in 1742, a member of a British scientific society saw a cylinder-shaped object with a lighted tail, that moved slowly above London. There were any number of mysterious flying objects seen over the United States in the 1890s, many of them well-documented sightings shared by hundreds of witnesses.

Since Kenneth Arnold's encounter with UFOs in 1947, there have been literally millions of sightings claimed, a fair number by experienced airline and military pilots. Many more people, or so it is believed, have seen UFOs, but are reticent about coming forward, fearing ridicule. A 1974 Gallup Poll in America put the national figure for people claiming to have seen a UFO at 11%. If true, this represents a figure of many millions of people. Another poll by the Opinion Research Corporation, found that only 13% of people who have seen a UFO, report it. The UFO Research Centre at Evanston, Illinois receive an average of 100 reports a night. One French computer scientist, after taking into account that most sightings take place at night when few people are up to watch them, and that some sightings are not reported, has calculated the number of 'landings' in the last 25 years as 3 000 000, which is a staggering figure.

Our world is only one of nine planets revolving around a star we call the Sun. The Sun in its turn is only one of millions of stars that make up our Galaxy. Beyond that there are millions of other stars in the vastness of space, each with their own attendant planets. Just how many planets are there on which intelligent life may exist? To say none is unrealistic. Scientists agree that life, or intelligence, is possible in other solar systems as well as our own. Man has only been an intelligent being, here on Earth, for little over 400 000 years, or so it is thought. Some scientific investigators are, however, beginning to question this, believing that man emerged much earlier. Who knows

how long intelligent beings have existed on other planets? Within other solar systems, intelligent life may well have mastered interstellar travel. Could they be visiting us?

Yet one serious stumbling block remains in the way of would-be believers in UFOs – the daunting statistics of space travel as we know it. First of all, assuming that there is intelligent life on one of the planets in orbit about Alpha Centauri, the nearest solar system to ours, it would take them 100 years travelling at over 112 654 000 kph to reach us. *The National Enquirer* in 1977 offered an award of $1 000 000 to anybody who could prove that UFOs come from outer space and are not natural pheno-

mena. Of course, no one has been able to provide this proof.

J Allen Hynek, an astronomer, has long argued that UFOs should be treated with an open mind:

'Everyone seems to have adopted some particular viewpoint. I know too much about the history of science not to know how dangerous that is. I go so far as to say, there is absolutely a UFO phenomenon. It is not all nonsense and misinterpretation. Then I simply say there are numerous hypotheses at present. It's a research problem.'

FLYING SAUCER REVIEW

Vol. 13, No. 6   November/December, 1967   13th Year of Publication

BRITAIN'S BUSIEST UFO DAYS

See Page 3

Could this scene from the film Star Wars *(left) be a real scene in the future? Although there is as yet no definite proof of life on other planets, many films, television programmes and books have been made about creatures and communities from somewhere in space. The UFO riddle is still unsolved but it is not forgotten, as this page from* Flying Saucer Review *shows.*

What happened to Buster Crabb?

With a practised flick of his flippers, the frogman dived for the second time that day.

The frogman tested his breathing equipment, then slapped his way flat-footed down the slimy dockside steps. It was still dark, but the lights flickering round Portsmouth Harbour and on the moored ships showed that the day had already begun. It was 19 April 1956. At the bottom of the steps the frogman turned, and with a skill born of long practice, dropped noiselessly into the water of the harbour. Shrugging off the cold, he began to swim leisurely on the surface towards the middle of the channel. 'Not the most pleasant place for an early-morning dip,' he thought to himself as he cut through the dirty, oil-slicked water which was covered with the usual flotsam and refuse that finds its way into a port.

Easily he made his way past the familiar landmarks and ships towards the entrance of the harbour. It was beginning to get light and by the time he reached Stokes Bay it was 7.30 am and broad daylight. It was a clear April morning and it looked like being a beautiful spring day. Anchored in the bay were three warships, a cruiser and two attendant destroyers. For a time, the frogman swam parallel with the ships taking in their unfamiliar silhouettes. Then, still on the surface, he headed between the two destroyers towards the cruiser. He was soon close enough to see the bustle on board as the ship began its day.

The nameplate stood out clearly: *Ordzhonikidze*. It was the crack Soviet cruiser that had brought Bulganin and Kruschev to Britain on a goodwill mission. With the easing of tension that had followed the end of the oppressive Stalin regime, the present Soviet leaders were putting out peace feelers in a series of visits to Western countries. With an eye to prestige, they had sailed aboard the ultra-modern *Ordzhonikidze*, the last word in cruiser design, crammed full of weaponry and detection equipment. The British Government, under Anthony Eden, had great hopes that the visit of Bulganin and 'Niki' Kruschev, all smiles and bonhomie, would go a long way to ending the 'cold war', and on their side they set out to promote a feeling of peace and goodwill in a series of frank and open discussions. So what was a frogman doing in Stokes Bay?

With a practised flick of his flippers, the frogman dived for the second time that day. He had had to surface after his first dive to report that his breathing apparatus was not working properly. This time he made his way through the murky water, a tell-tale stream of bubbles marking the direction of his progress. That was the last to be seen of Commander Lionel K P Crabb RNVR (Royal Naval Volunteer Reserve), Buster to his friends.

The Russian leaders, Bulganin and Kruschev, with Anthony Eden. They were in Britain on a goodwill mission. With an eye to prestige, they arrived aboard the modern Russian cruiser Ordzhonikidze.

Why was an expert diver operating around one of the newest and most deadly fighting ships in the world? Had he been sent to spy on the underwater equipment of the *Ordzhonikidze*? If so, who had sent him? On the surface it would seem unlikely that the British Government would jeopardize the goodwill talks for the sake of relatively unimportant information, however interesting, and carry out the operation in broad daylight in sight of two other Russian ships. Or had someone blundered?

Commander Buster Crabb was a character. A small man, 1.67 metres tall, he had started life as an apprentice in the Merchant Navy. At the end of his time he took a shore job with an American oil company. At the outbreak of the Second World War in 1939, he immediately volunteered for service with the Merchant Navy, acting as a gunner aboard a tanker. He

Schoolchildren pose with Buster Crabb.

was then 29. Eventually, he received a commission in the RNVR and was posted to Gibraltar, the British Naval base at the entrance to the Mediterranean. It was while acting as a bomb and mine disposal officer on the Rock in 1942, that he found his true vocation. Always a keen swimmer, he took to underwater diving with the greatest ease and was soon regarded as something of an expert in this field.

It was a tricky, dangerous job which he had undertaken, protecting shipping against any underwater attacks by the Italian midget sub- marines and manned torpedoes. The Italians had been the first to pioneer this form of undersea warfare and their courageous crews had already put two British battleships, *Valiant* and *Queen Elizabeth*, out of action as they lay moored in Alexandria Harbour in Egypt. Then the Italians concentrated on Gibraltar. The Battle of the Mediterranean was dragging on and the convoys assembled at the Rock for the final run to Malta made a tempting target. Crabb and his team of frogmen saved tens of thousands of tons of shipping and hundreds of lives.

Was Buster Crabb among this crowd, watching as the Soviet cruiser, Ordzhonikidze *sailed into Portsmouth Harbour?*

A man with a reputation for being able to handle tricky situations, Crabb was called to assist in the Truculent *rescue operation. Here she is beached on Cheney Spit off Sheerness after being raised.*

Buster Crabb ended the war as a Lieutenant-Commander, with a reputation for being able to handle tricky situations and get out of tight corners. Leaving the Navy, he did a number of underwater jobs for the Admiralty as a civilian, but he missed being in the Navy and later rejoined, specializing in undersea rescue. He helped rescue some of the crew of the submarine *Truculent*, and also took part in the search for the ill-fated *Affray*. He finally retired officially in 1955 with the rank of Commander. Unofficially he still retained connections with Naval Intelligence. It was rumoured that he had carried out a mission for them when the Soviet cruiser *Sverdlov* was in Portsmouth in the autumn of 1955, on a goodwill visit. He was presumably asked to inspect the hull for secret underwater equipment.

Crabb booked into Portsmouth's Sallyport Hotel on 17 April 1956 – or so it is thought – with a younger man Bernard Smith. The following day Crabb left the hotel early in the morning, and returned late evening. No one knew what he had been doing, or where he had been. He was again seen leaving the hotel in the early hours of the morning of 19 April – alone. Bernard Smith left later in the day paying both bills and taking Crabb's luggage with him. Despite exhaustive enquiries this man was never traced. His identity and his reason for being with Crabb still remains a mystery. Some people believe he was an American; others

think he was an agent of the British Special Intelligence Service. The mystery deepened when, several days later, an officer of the Special Branch paid the hotel a visit, questioning the staff about Crabb and his friend. After removing the pages of the hotel register relevant to Crabb's stay, the detective left, cautioning the hotel manager and his staff with the Official Secrets Act. Under no circumstances were they to discuss the matter with anybody.

Meanwhile, some of Buster Crabb's naval friends, worried that he had failed to turn up in his usual haunts for several days, approached the Admiralty. On 29 April, the Admiralty issued a brief statement:

'He is presumed to be dead as a result of trials with certain underwater apparatus. The location was in Stokes Bay, and it is nine days since the accident.'

There was no mention of his body being recovered; no mention of the nature of the trials. The cat was out of the bag and the press, sensing a good story, gave it banner headlines on 30 April: 'Missing Frogman Mystery'.

Crabb also took part in the search for the Affray.

Radar-equipped Boxer *searching for the* Affray.

Of all places, why were the trials carried out in Stokes Bay in the vicinity of a new Soviet cruiser? In view of the goodwill mission it was political dynamite. The wardrooms and pubs of Portsmouth buzzed with rumour. Those who knew Buster Crabb well, and other frogmen who were aware of his capabilities, dismissed the idea of an accident. They took the line that he had been killed by the Russians while inspecting the hull of the *Ordzhonikidze*, and that his corpse had been taken aboard to be jettisoned on the voyage home.

Press reports became more sensational and dockyard rumour-mongers spread the most unlikely stories. One such story said that Crabb was still alive, a prisoner on one of the Russian ships which had sailed on 28 April taking back the Soviet leaders. Once in Moscow he would be interrogated for the invaluable information he possessed. Another story hinted that Crabb was not working for Britain, but for a foreign power, and the American accent of his companion at the Sallyport Hotel pointed a finger at the Central Intelligence Agency.

No, another said, Buster was not spying on the Soviet cruiser. On the contrary, he was protecting it from sabotage by a group of anarchists intent on causing an international incident. Others said he allowed himself to be seen diving near the Russian ships to obtain publicity for a book he was writing. Moving into the realms of fantasy, it was even suggested that his naval friends had recovered his body from the harbour and buried him secretly at night with full military honours.

Sensitive to the sensational press reports, the Soviet Government instructed their Embassy in London to send a note to the Foreign Office on 4 May:

'During the stay of Soviet ships at Portsmouth, at 7.30 am on 19 April seamen on board a Soviet ship observed a frogman floating between the Soviet destroyers. The frogman, who wore a black diving suit with flippers on his feet, was seen on the surface of the water for one to three minutes and then he dived again. . . . The commanding officer of the Soviet ships, Rear Admiral Kotov, in a conversation with the Chief of Staff of the Portsmouth naval base, Rear Admiral Burnett, drew his attention to the case. Rear Admiral Burnett categorically rejected the possibility . . . and stated, at the time indicated, there were no operations in the port involving the use of frogmen.'

The press went on to make political capital out of the unfortunate announcement previously made by the Admiralty. As they pointed out, this announcement did not align with Rear Admiral Burnett's categorical rejection of the possibility of a frogman being in Stokes Bay. Would the British Government give 'an explanation of this matter'? The goodwill built up from the B and K visit, as the press termed it, looked to be in some jeopardy.

The official reply from the Foreign Office did little to clear the matter up, but it soothed Russian indignation. It was more than possible that the frogman was Commander Crabb, but:

'his presence in the vicinity of the destroyers occurred without any permission whatever and Her Majesty's Government express their regret for the incident.'

So far so good. But the Opposition in the House of Commons had no intention of letting sleeping dogs lie. The Prime Minister was questioned by an Opposition Member:
'What were the circumstances under which Commander Crabb disappeared?'
Anthony Eden gave the time-honoured answer of a senior politician under pressure: '. . . it would not be in the public interest to disclose the circumstances . . .'

This had the Leader of the Opposition, Hugh Gaitskell, leaping to his feet. 'Would the Prime Minister enlarge on the answer he had already given, and assure us . . .'

The Prime Minister would not. Pouncing upon what they believed to be an embarrassment for the Government, the Opposition made another attempt to drive Anthony Eden into a corner on 14 May. But the Prime Minister would not be drawn, declaring '. . . that no government in any country would say more than I am prepared to say . . .' The national interest would not gain by discussing certain matters of security.

This rather ham-fisted way of dealing with the situation left most people in no doubt that something odd had happened, and that the authorities knew far more about the situation than they were prepared to admit. But like all items of news value it quickly faded from the newspapers and was forgotten.

Then in October 1956 a report came from a news agency in Copenhagen. Russian seamen who had been aboard the *Ordzhonikidze* at Portsmouth in April of the previous year had stated that someone had been held under guard in a sealed-off part of the cruiser's sick bay, but they had no idea who this was. It raised only a faint murmur of interest.

In May 1957, this statement from a senior Whitehall official gave rise to another crop of rumours:

Fishermen Randall and Gilbey, who found the body.

'We are satisfied that Commander Crabb did not die when he went into the water at Portsmouth near the Russian warships. We have good reason to believe that he was taken aboard one of the ships and is now being held in Russia.'

It now looked as if the B and K goodwill mission had not been quite the success expected. Once more the newspapers took up the story:

'Is Crabb Alive?'

Dead on cue an answer was provided. On 9 June 1957, a group of fishermen came across a body floating in the sea near the entrance to Chichester Harbour. As the body had neither head nor hands, identification was going to prove difficult. It was established at an inquest held on 11 June, that the body had been in the water for a considerable time, at least six and possibly 14 months – an odd and seemingly arbitrary time scale to choose.

The facts were martialled:

1 Commander Crabb had disappeared 14 months previously.
2 A doctor gave it as his opinion that the corpse was that of a man 1.67 metres in height – Commander Crabb was 1.67 metres tall.
3 Chichester police were of the opinion that coastal currents would carry a corpse from Stokes Bay in the direction of Chichester Harbour.
4 The corpse had a scar on its left knee – Crabb had received an injury during the war which had left him with a similar scar.
5 The corpse was wearing a two-piece diving suit of the kind supplied to Commander Crabb, who did not like the one-piece naval issue.
6 The Corpse had deformed toes – Crabb was hammer-toed, but his toes had been more deformed than those of the corpse.

The coroner brought in an open verdict – death from unknown causes. He made it clear that, although there were discrepancies:

'Looking at the evidence in this case, I am quite satisfied that the remains which were found in Chichester Harbour on 9 June were those of Commander Crabb.'

No mention was made of the missing head and hands. Might it be that the authorities were being over-hasty in covering up what after all was an embarrassing situation? The body was buried at Milton cemetery and there the matter would probably have rested, had someone not remembered that three Soviet submarines had passed up the English Channel on their way to Egypt only three days before the body had been found.

Once more the newshounds were hot on the scent and the Crabb story was resurrected. One school of thought favoured the idea that the Russians, reacting to the reports, had killed Crabb and dropped him overboard from one of the submarines as it cruised past Portsmouth. There are three arguments against this however. Firstly, the Soviet submarines were under observation, certainly radar observation and most probably visual (shadowing submarines etc), from the very first moment they entered the English Channel. In which case there is a strong possibility that they would have been seen jettisoning the body. Would the

Soviet Government risk an international incident and world-wide loss of face just to allay press rumours? Secondly, the body would not have been in anything like the advanced state of decomposition that it was in, if it had been thrown overboard only three days previously, unless the Russians had kept it in water for many months, but why on earth should they do that? Finally, if the Russians wanted the matter closed once and for all, and Crabb's body positively identified, then why did they cut off the head and hands?

A second theory offered at the time seems more likely. A body similar to Crabb's was kept in water for all those months then, when the opportunity arose, it was dropped off Portsmouth by one of the three Soviet submarines. The head and hands were cut off because they had identifying features that would make it obvious that the body was not that of Commander Crabb.

Far fetched? Possibly, but the British did a similar thing during the Second World War to deceive the German General Staff. A body was dropped from a submarine off the coast of Spain, having been kept preserved in ice for a number of weeks. This was the same principle, but in reverse. If this were true it could only mean one thing. Crabb was still alive and in Russian hands, and there was a strong possibility that he had defected to the other side of the Iron Curtain.

It would seem that the whole truth about Commander Buster Crabb has yet to be told. Will we ever know what happened to him that April morning in Stokes Bay? Will the true facts behind the British Government's statements ever come to light?

The Miracle Healer

He then plunged a stainless steel kitchen knife into the man's left eye, and began to scrape and probe.

The village of Congonhas do Campo sits in a fold of the mountain plateau in the State of Minas Gerais, the rich mining area of Brazil. The fame of this small village had, until 1963, rested with works of a mysterious 18th century sculptor, Aleijadinho, whose statues today draw visitors from all over the world. Life-size figures of the twelve Biblical prophets, carved in soapstone, stand as sentinels on the terrace of the church of Bom Jesus, overlooking the village. Over 60 life-size figures, carved in cedar, of Christ and the Crucifixion are housed in small chapels in the hilly garden of the church. These statues, both wooden and stone, are so vivid and life-like that they have a profound effect on both visitors and villagers alike. Aleijadinho, crippled with leprosy, had strapped tools to his withered stumps of arms and patiently chipped away at his statues. Yet his work is magnificently precise and emotionally overpowering – minor miracles! But other miracles were being performed in this village in 1963.

The peasant squatting against the rough-plastered wall sent his cigarette end spinning into the dusty gutter. Already at 7 o'clock in the morning the hot Brazilian sun was beating down on the cobblestoned street called Rua Marechal Floriano. About 200 people were jostling in the narrow street behind the peasant, many had been there since before sunrise. They were waiting for the doors of a strange clinic to open – a clinic housed in a dilapidated former church. An old blind peasant, leaning heavily on a stick, rubbed shoulders with an elegantly-dressed aristocratic lady in her forties. A pale, skinny man with an enormous goitre in his neck grumbled at a fat negress holding a not too-clean handkerchief to her eyes. A small, wan child in a wheelchair stared wistfully into space – his mother standing guard, watching over their place in the queue that now stretched down the Rua Marechal Floriano and round the corner. This motley collection, from every walk of life, had come from all over Brazil and other countries in South America, converging on Congonhas do Campo by bus, train and family car. More than a few had arrived in Cadillacs and expensive Mercedes. Some were garrulous, others stood mute, but they shared a sense of expectancy, and blind faith hung in the morning air as thick as a blanket.

The doors opened and the crowd began to stream in. The clinic was open. But everyone knew that today was something different. Word had gone around the village that two Americanos had arrived to watch the clinic in action. They made an unlikely team. The elder of the two, Henry Belk, was a southerner from North Carolina. A successful business man, he had set up an extensive foundation to research into the para-normal. His companion, Dr Henry Puharich, a specialist in bio-engineering, was an active man in his forties with a decided interest in psychic phenomena. He had been drawn together with Belk in the investigation of a medium with considerable powers of ESP (extrasensory perception). Now the two men found themselves in a remote Brazilian village investigating an even stranger happening. So far they were not very impressed. A 12-hour drive in a minibus had left them tired and disgruntled, and a night spent in a small, sleazy hotel had done nothing to sweeten their tempers, and now this broken-down church in a seedy village. They were hardly in a receptive mood to approach any scientific enquiry in a detached, unbiased manner. With them were two interpreters from the University of Rio de Janeiro as neither of them spoke Portuguese.

As the four men arrived at the doors of the church they were waved into the clinic ahead of the staring patients, by a softly-spoken dark-skinned man who told them that his name was Altimiro. Inside they were greeted by a powerful-looking man in a dark shirt and trousers. He had a heavy, black moustache and a thick mop of equally black hair. But it was his eyes that drew the attention of the Americans. They were sharp and piercing. So this was Arigo, the man they had travelled thousands of kilometres to see at work. He was certainly not what they expected. A cross between a peasant farm labourer and a truck driver, he scarcely fitted the role of psychic surgeon, by now a living legend in Brazil. Arigo greeted them warmly and led them into a barn-like room with pale green plaster walls. There were wooden benches round the walls and down the centre of the room, which were crowded with patients nervously awaiting their turn for treatment. Other patients leaned against the walls. Leading off this room was a cubicle with just a crude

wooden table and chair inside. On one wall there was a crucifix, on another a picture of Christ. This was where Arigo worked.

The two Americans looked at each other. To them the scene was strange and unreal, and it had an air of both expectancy and despair. Several of the patients glanced uneasily in their direction as Arigo stepped into the centre of the room. The interpreters translated his Portuguese, which he spoke with a rough peasant accent.

'All religions are good,' he said. 'Is this not so?'

Jose Arigo, guided by the spirit of a surgeon.

There was a murmur of assent from the crowded room. It was not he but Jesus who brought about the cures he told them. The next moment he was condemning smoking and alcohol, and saying that drinking and gambling were the curse of men, along with lying and cheating. Then he led the room in prayer. Embarrassed, the Americans were by now convinced that they had come to Congonhas do Campo on a wild-goose chase. Two young female assistants moved about the room arranging the patients in a line facing Arigo's cubicle which he had entered alone. The Americans' softly-spoken guide sat in a corner, in front of an ancient typewriter. They had no idea why.

Arigo stepped from his cubicle, but he was a completely different Arigo. His eyes, radiantly penetrating yet somehow remote, glittered in the dim light. His bearing was almost arrogant. He now spoke in a commanding voice with, according to the interpreters, a thick German accent, harsh and gutteral. He ordered the Americans into his cubicle and they followed like lambs.

'There is nothing to hide here,' he said. 'I am happy to have you watch. I must assure you that what I do is safe, and that the people who are ill become well.' He was no longer a peasant, but a man used to command.

Without ceremony, he roughly pushed his

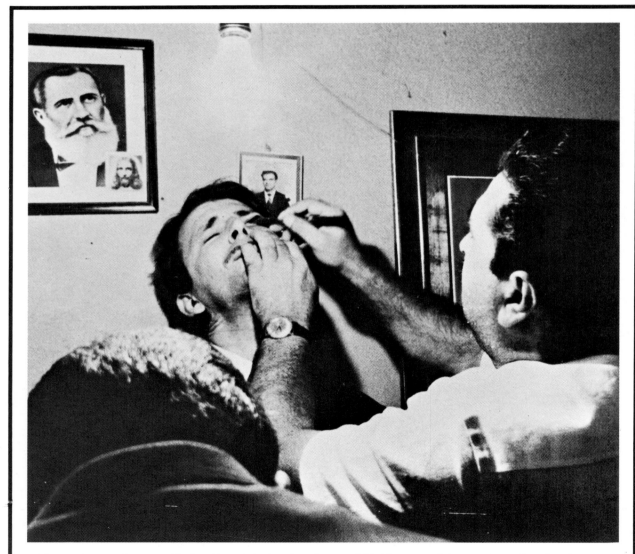

Many witnesses have testified to Jose Arigo's miraculous and highly successful operations. Here he plunges a kitchen knife into a man's left eye socket and begins to scrape and probe.

first patient, an elderly well-dressed man, against the wall. He then plunged a stainless steel kitchen paring knife into the man's left eye, deep into the eye socket, and began to scrape and probe. Shocked, Puharich and Belk could only gape in stunned silence. One woman screamed, another fainted, but the patient, fully conscious, stood calm and relaxed, showing no fear. He neither moved nor flinched, other than to flick a fly from his cheek. Arigo invited Puharich to place his finger on the eyelid to feel the point of the knife. Sick with shock he did so; it was all too real. This turned out to be Arigo's method of diagnosing eye complaints and it took him less than a minute. Afterwards, the patient, who had received no anaesthetic, hypnotic or otherwise, told them that although he had been aware of the knife, he had felt no pain or discomfort.

Pausing only to wipe the knife on his sports shirt, Arigo undertook operation after operation with lightning speed, here removing a cyst, there a tumour. One woman had a large goitre removed in a matter of seconds. There was hardly any bleeding and the incisions were small by normal surgical standards, often smaller than the growths removed. Sometimes, with a single glance at the patient, Arigo would scribble a prescription to be typed at machine-gun speed by his assistant.

Still in a state of shock and unable to believe the evidence of their own eyes, the two Americans recalled what they had been told back in Rio. They had heard that Arigo claimed to be controlled by the spirit of a German doctor, Adolpho Fritz, who had died in 1918. It was this Dr Fritz who directed the surgery and made the instant diagnoses. Arigo, one of eight brothers, sons of a small farmer, was born on 18 October, 1921. Although by and large leading a normal childhood, at school he claimed to have been bothered by 'a bright round light, so bright that it nearly blinded me.' Then he began hearing 'a voice that spoke in a strange language,' but not often and he learned to put up with it. When he was twenty-five he married Arlete Andre, a fourth cousin, left his father's farm and took a job in a local iron mine.

As children began to arrive in rapid succession, Arigo started having persistent dreams. They were disturbing and often accompanied by blinding headaches from which he could get no relief. In these dreams, he heard the same gutteral voice talking to him in a language he could not understand. One night he had a particularly vivid dream. He was in an operating theatre where there were doctors and nurses wearing old-fashioned surgical gowns grouped round a patient. Directing the operation was a bald, stout man whose voice was all too familiar to Arigo.

Night after night the same dream returned, and after a time the central figure of his nightmare introduced himself as Dr Adolpho Fritz. He had died during the First World War and his work on Earth had not been completed. He went on to tell Arigo that he had chosen him as a living medium to carry on his work. Other spirits who had been doctors before they died would also help. If Arigo was to find peace he must devote himself to curing the sick and afflicted.

Waking with a start, Arigo leaped out of bed and ran screaming, stark naked, into the street. Gently he had to be led back to the house, weeping bitterly. The family doctor sent him for tests, both medical and psychological. The specialists found him perfectly fit and mentally normal, but still the dreams and blinding headaches persisted. The village priest tried, but could not help. His attempt at exorcism (by now he thought Arigo was possessed) was a total failure. Driven by his unfortunate situation, Arigo decided to see what would happen if he gave in to the German doctor's demands. Meeting a friend of his, a cripple forced to hobble about on crutches, Arigo found himself blurting out, 'It's about time you got rid of those crutches.' Snatching them away he told the man to walk, which he did and continued to do so.

It so happened at this time that a Brazilian senator, Lucio Bittencourt, was campaigning in the district for re-election. He was also deeply involved in promoting Gelulio Vargas, a presidential candidate representing the Brazilian Workers Party. Doctors had diagnosed that Bittencourt had lung cancer, and gave their opinion that an operation, preferably in the United States, should be carried out immediately. Secretly they had little hope of the outcome. Committed to the cause of Vargas, Bittencourt had decided to postpone surgery until after the campaign had ended. He met Arigo, an ex-union leader at the iron mine, when he visited Congonhas do Campo and, impressed by his magnetism, he invited Arigo to attend a rally in nearby Belo Horizonte. The two men, staying at the same hotel, spent a convivial evening drinking frothy, dark Brazilian beer with party workers.

Later, as Bittencourt lay on his bed staring at the ceiling, desperately worried about his illness, he saw the bedroom door begin to open slowly. A shadowy figure he thought to be Arigo came into the room and switched on the light. It was Arigo, standing quite still with an open razor in his hand, his eyes glazed and remote. Amazed, the senator tried to sit up, but a strange faintness overcame him and he fell back. Everything became blurred and he blacked out. Next morning he awoke to find his pyjamas slashed across the back and covered in dried blood. In the mirror he could see a neat incision in his back just below the ribcage, the blood already congealing. The cancer had been removed and it was confirmed later that the senator was completely cured.

41

Arigo, despite persecution by the Church and the authorities, set up a clinic where he treated up to 200 patients a day – more than a large, well-equipped hospital could treat in a month, and continued to do so until that day in 1963.

After observing Arigo working in his clinic for two days Dr Puharich came to a decision. Somehow, he and Belk must set Arigo a positive test under control conditions and make a colour film of it. Jorge Rizzini, who had been chiefly responsible for bringing Arigo to the attention of the Brazilian public, was a journalist and documentary film maker in São Paulo. He had already made a number of colour films of the psychic surgeon's operations, and he offered to film, in colour, anything that the Americans judged to be conclusive evidence. But how to select something immediately believable that would convince even the most sceptical viewer?

Now, Dr Puharich had had a non-malignant tumour called a lipoma for the last seven years. It was located on the inside of his right elbow, and although not painful, it was an unsightly nuisance. It was over 3·5 centimetres long, 12 millimetres wide, and 12 millimetres deep. Normal surgery to remove it would take from 15 to 20 minutes. It would be a tricky operation too, as the lipoma lay directly above the ulnar nerve which controls the use of the hand, and one careless slip of the scalpel would cause the doctor to lose the use of his fingers on that hand.

After hours of agonizing indecision, Dr Puharich decided to ask Arigo to remove the lipoma. A good film of this must remove any doubts in the minds of both Belk and himself, as well as going a long way to convince outside authorities. Arigo agreed and all the necessary preparations for filming were made. When the doctor arrived at the clinic the next morning, Arigo turned to the room already crowded with patients and asked, 'Has anybody here got a good Brazilian pocket knife to use on this Americano?' Horrified as he was, Puharich could hardly turn back. Knives were offered from every direction. Arigo chose a particularly villainous-looking knife and then turned to Puharich.

'Roll up your sleeve, doctor.'

Nervously, the American checked the camera set-up. Rizzini intended to bounce his battery light off the ceiling to eliminate the possibility of burning out the image. The camera was in position.

'Look away,' said Arigo.

Seconds later Puharich felt something soft in his hand along with the pocket knife. It was the lipoma. He looked down at his arm and saw that where the tumour had been was now quite flat. There was just a slight incision, less than 5 centimetres long, and a slight trickle of blood. Arigo had scraped the knife over the surface of the skin and it was all over. The doctor had felt only a vague sensation, and later said

'I experienced absolutely zero. I couldn't believe this had happened, yet it had, and there was no mistake about it.'

No infection followed the surgery and the wound healed completely.

Rizzini's film was clear and well-exposed. It showed that the whole operation had lasted only five seconds. Belk and Puharich, two sceptical investigators, were utterly convinced. Arigo continued to practise and never accepted payment for his services.

Claim after claim poured into the offices of the Brazilian newspapers and journals. The wife of Virgilio Medes Feraz, one of the richest men in the country, was cured of cancer by Arigo. So was her friend, Ismenio Silveiro, after surgery in one of the best hospitals in South America had been unsuccessful. Arigo quickly diagnosed that the daughter of the Brazilian President, Kubitschek, had two massive stones in the kidneys, and so the list goes on. Countless hundreds of people were prepared to testify to the miraculous cures of Arigo. A vast case book was built up on him showing startling success in every branch of medicine and surgery. Yet still the authorities hounded him. Twice he was put on trial, but he still carried on his mission. Gradually he won through until it seemed that at last his work would be recognized officially, not only in Brazil, but in the rest of the world.

It was at this time, the time of his triumph, that Arigo, dreaming of a black crucifix, was convinced that he was shortly going to meet with a violent end. On 11 June, 1971, he went to his clinic as usual, but he informed his patients that he had to go to a neighbouring town to pick up a second-hand car. In heavy rain Arigo set off. Jose Timoteo, of the National Highway Department, was driving a heavy pick-up truck. Rounding a hairpin bend on a precipitous mountain road, he was horrified to see a blue car move across the road towards him. It was not skidding, but turning straight into his path. He stood on his brakes, but to no avail, the two vehicles smashed into each other with a crash that was heard over 1 kilometre away. Arigo was dead!

Brazil is a strange country. Almost as big as the whole of the United States of America, it is a country in which Indian, Negro and Catholic mysticism has been fused; a country which claims to have not one but numerous Arigos.

The Gloucester Sea Serpent

For 15 minutes the sea serpent kept pace with the ship, undulating through the water with an easy grace, and seeming totally unconcerned.

It had been a successful trip and the New England whaler, her holds crammed with casks of oil, was spanking along before a brisk six-knot breeze. On her port bow the lights of Cape Cod marked the ship's entrance into the Gulf of Maine. They would soon be home. The season had been a gruelling one, but the Lord had been kind. Whales had been plentiful and they had lost only one whale boat and two hands. The widows would receive their share. Hard-bitten, the whalers were tough but God-fearing. Whaling in the Antarctic was demanding, as the seamen had to have their wits about them at all times. Spotting drifting ice and the more sinister 'blue' icebergs became a matter of life or death. Ship-wrecked, a man could not last more than two minutes in the icy waters of the South. Lookouts developed almost a sixth sense. They could spot a berg or a whale far off on the horizon in any conditions, and their reaction was instantaneous and accurate.

It was the summer of 1817 and through the early morning haze, the lookout could see the coast of Massachusetts looming dead ahead. They were no more than a few kilometres from Gloucester, their home port. Already the crew, weary of the bitterly cold grey wastes of the southern seas, were crowding the fore rails, hungry for a glimpse of their home town. They would make the occasional trip to the grog shop to swap yarns with other whaling men, and the money shared from the sale of their cargo would keep them and their families clothed and fed until next season's whaling.

Did the Gloucester sea serpent really look like this late 19th-century impression?

They were just coming in to port when the lookout shouted down to his mates lining the forepeak. 'There's something big moving off the starboard bow.' Even from his position in the crow's nest it was difficult for him to make out what it was. Something huge was churning the sea into a frenzy. If it was a whale rising it was the biggest he had ever seen, and whales were unknown off the coast of New England at this time of year. Suddenly a monstrous coil rose from the water, then another. Below, silent with superstitious fear, the hardened whalers could only stare. No one ran for a harpoon, which was a natural reaction in the Antarctic.

Less than 200 metres away a ghastly serpent-like head broke the surface. Panic-stricken, the lookout scurried down the rigging, while the cry, 'Monster' ran through the ship. The crew quickly put on full sail and the whaler fairly flew for the safety of the harbour. For 15 minutes the sea serpent, such they took it to be, kept pace with the ship, undulating through the water with an easy grace, and seeming totally unconcerned. Then, to the relief of the badly frightened crew, it dropped astern and slid beneath the waves.

They tied up and the usual crowd were waiting to greet them on the jetty. Husbands waved to their wives and children as they hastened down the gangway, loaded with kitbags and hammocks. But it was a sheepish crew who greeted their loved ones. Should they mention the monster? Would they be believed? They need not have worried, as the sea serpent was the talk of the New England coast. Already innumerable sightings had been reported and the citizens of Gloucester rushed to the beaches to catch a glimpse of the mysterious creature as it slid silently through the water off their town. For it seemed only to patrol in the vicinity of Gloucester and nearby monster-haunted Nahant Bay. There were no serious reports from elsewhere along the coast. The only previous report of a sea serpent had come from John Josselyn, who had visited Nahant Bay in 1638. He described the monster as being seen, 'quoiled up on a rock at Cape Ann.'

As always in such cases the descriptions of the monster were varied, confused and conflicting, often depending on the amount of rum consumed by the observer. However, it was

This early 19th-century engraving of the serpent looks unlikely to be true to life. However, records show that the people who sought the reward for its capture believed it existed.

generally believed to be about 30 metres long and 1 metre in diameter. Most people agreed that the serpent had a smooth shiny skin, either black or dark brown in colour, and a few claimed to have seen a remarkably long tongue. One old salt maintained that it had the eye of an ox, but this might have been due to the rum. The creature was usually seen idling in the waves, though on occasions it appeared to glide rapidly through the water with a powerful arching of its sinuous back.

Gloucester is the next village to Salem, a few kilometres down the coast, and it too had a history of sightings during the 18th century. So, when the serpent appeared 100 years later, it would have been taken very seriously. In the event, a large reward was posted for its capture, dead or alive.

As the fame of the monster spread, people flocked into Gloucester hoping to spot the sea serpent. The more adventurous of them even had the temerity to venture out in small boats to try for a close look. Whaling boats set out from Gloucester with their harpoon men perched in the bows, the crews anxious for the reward despite the risk. Fishermen even tried to net the monster. The situation became serious enough for the American Naval authorities to intervene, and they despatched a revenue cutter to patrol the area with guns at the ready. One witness claimed to have got close enough to the serpent to empty his duck gun at its head, but without result.

Apparently, the monster was oblivious to the consternation it was causing, totally ignoring its audience, whether hostile or curious. Nor did it ever make any sound. For a period of two weeks it terrorized the Gloucester shore, then suddenly it disappeared. It was last seen moving south towards Nahant Bay, and reappeared for its final curtain call in Long Island Sound.

Kidd's Treasure

The pirates struggled up the rock and lowered the chests carefully into the water, one by one.

Captain Kidd. There is no evidence to show that he was a cold-blooded villain.

Kidd's treasure conjures up visions of chest upon iron-bound chest, stuffed with pieces of eight, bars of silver, diamonds, emeralds, rubies, sapphires and pearls; all the ill-gotten gains of a lifetime spent marauding on the Spanish Main. Captain William Kidd has become a legend, along with his treasure, as a ferocious pirate who terrorized the sea lanes of the world – the scourge of every honest merchant.

The *Adventure* was wallowing at anchor in a slight swell off Skeleton Island, somewhere north of the Philippines in the China Sea. The crew were anxious for the captain to get his business over quickly so that they could head into the Indian Ocean for the Cape of Good Hope and home. They were only too well aware of the reputation of their present anchorage. Known as the 'Father of Typhoons' by the natives, the area was subject to sudden violent storms and the *Adventure* was in no shape to weather one of those.

'Lower the longboat,' called the bosun.

Ropes squealed in the wooden blocks as the ship's boat swung outboard, hitting the water with a smack. The boat's crew scurried over the side and manned the oars. Carefully the heavy iron-bound chests were lowered into the boat and stowed aft. Then the mate clambered down, followed by the captain, William Kidd. Kidd stood in the stern, his floppy hat keeping the sun out of his eyes, a heavy musket on one shoulder and another thrust into his wide cummerbund. 'You never know who you'll find on an island,' he told the crew. It was 1697 and Kidd and his men were going ashore to bury the wealth, believed at that time to be worth £250 000, stolen from Prince Aurengzeb, Great Mogul and Sovereign of India. The pirates dug their oars into the oily swell and the longboat glided towards the tiny island – uninhabited they had always been led to believe, but the captain was usually right.

As the prow of the boat crunched into the sand, the crew leaped out and dragged it above the water mark.

'You men carry the chests, the mate and I'll carry the muskets. Head for that clump of palms.'

Soon they were deep in the jungle, their shirts clinging to their backs in the sticky heat. They had no idea which way they were going and the captain didn't seem to be taking bearings. After an hour's march the trees began to thin out and they found themselves in a steep-sided valley. Kidd christened it The Valley of Death. At the head of the valley, past a tree of peculiar shape, lay a small lake, about 5 fathoms (9 metres) deep.

'We'll stow the treasure here, lads,' called Kidd. 'Drop the chests off that rock, it's deep enough.'

The pirates, eager to get rid of the heavy chests, struggled up the rock and lowered them carefully into the water, one by one. They stood intently watching each chest sink to the muddy bottom of the lake. When they turned, they found themselves facing two muskets.

'Sorry, lads.' A flash of flame and two of the boat's crew lay dead – shot at point blank range. Two others made a dash for the woods, only to be calmly shot down by the mate. The two remaining men ran at Kidd but he shot one, and ran the other through with his cutlass. 'Well, lad,' he said to the mate, 'they'll never tell.'

Then the even more grisly task began. Kidd and the mate dragged the bodies away one at a time and crucified each of them to a tree leading to the treasure, their right arms pointing in the direction of the hiding place. The job done, Kidd and his lieutenant made their way back to the longboat and dragged it to the water's edge. The captain jumped in first. 'Shove her off, lad,' he said to the mate.

The mate exerted all his strength, the boat began to float, and Kidd shot the mate straight between the eyes with his other musket. Now only he knew where the treasure was buried.

Legend does not record what the rest of the pirate crew had to say when the captain turned up alone, but the story was sufficient to send any number of treasure hunters out to the China Sea in search of Kidd's fabulous hoard. But there is one thing seriously wrong with this story. William Kidd was just not that sort of man. There is absolutely no evidence to show he was a cold-blooded villain, but there is almost certainly a treasure buried somewhere.

William Kidd, thought to have been born in Greenock, Scotland, in about 1645, was a sea captain who owned a fleet of trading vessels. Modestly well-off, he lived in some style with his family in New York in America. When William III came to the throne of England in 1689, he commissioned Kidd to suppress piracy, then rife on the high seas, and if possible bring to Execution Dock the four most notorious of the pirate captains: Thomas Tew, Thomas Wake, William Maze and John Ireland. Although the king addressed Kidd as 'his dear friend', he failed to offer him adequate and guaranteed payment for the job. He left it to the 'man on the spot', Lord Bellemont, to agree with the captain a percentage of 'all captures made on board pirate vessels'. What is more, the expedition was financed by a private company and not by the British Government. Lord Bellemont and his cronies could scent a fine profit.

Governor Fletcher of New York with Captain Tew, one of the pirates that Kidd was commissioned to capture.

Kidd's ship, the *Adventure*, a frigate with a crew of 155 and armed with four cannons, first sailed south-eastwards to Madeira, then on to Cape Verde and round the Cape of Good Hope into the Indian Ocean. At the time, pirates haunted this ocean, preying on the richly-laden East Indiamen on their sluggish voyage home to Britain. For months on end the *Adventure* cruised off Madagascar, now called Malagasy, and the coast of Africa without ever sighting a single pirate vessel. Constant revictualling and renewal of equipment – sails, cordage, blocks and tackle and all the other things required aboard a sailing ship – were eating up the available money. As a policing exercise it was a disaster. Wherever the *Adventure* went, the pirates always seemed to be somewhere else. Their intelligence would have appeared to be better than Kidd's. There was nothing for it but to return to New York and admit failure, not an easy thing for a man of Kidd's temperament to stomach. He dreaded to think what Lord Belle-mont and his friends would say. Why, he'd be the laughing stock of New York.

Tempers were on edge and nerves at breaking point, when an incident took place which did much to change Kidd's attitude to the voyage of the *Adventure*. At his wit's end, not knowing which way to turn, Kidd was provoked into a quarrel by William Moore, the chief gunner. Blind with rage, the captain smashed a heavy wooden pail over the gunner's head. Next day the man died from a broken skull. Gradually Kidd and his crew slipped into a lax moral attitude towards their task. Their definition of pirates became more elastic, and they began to turn to piracy themselves. Their first victim was a Moorish ship which they stopped and boarded on the thin excuse that all Moors were pirates. Kidd battled with his conscience, but egged on by his crew he began to stop other ships on the flimsiest of pretexts, and after a while the master and crew of the *Adventure* needed no excuse at all. The treasure and rich cargoes taken were mounting up, and with the seizure of the *Quedagh Merchant*, a fine vessel of about 500 tons, the pirates decided to rest up, assess their loot and share it according to the time honoured rules of piracy.

Kidd now thought it time to destroy the *Adventure*, which was too well known as a pirate ship and was badly in need of cleaning and repair. So when he next put to sea it was aboard the *Quedagh Merchant*.

Having divided the spoils – piastres, silver coins, diamonds, rubies and gold to the value of £400 000 – they now had the problem of getting it back to New York, and what's more, explain where it had come from. The rich cargo in the hold was no problem. This valuable merchandise of spices, silk, sugar and saltpetre, would be shared out among the backers. Lord Bellemont and his cronies would be more than satisfied with such a haul. Kidd fondly seemed to believe that his piracy had gone unnoticed. Anyway, he could always rely on the protection of the English king and his influential backers.

In October 1698, the *Quedagh Merchant* rounded the Cape of Good Hope and headed across the Atlantic to America. Calling at Anguilla, in the West Indies, on the way, the crew hastened ashore to do the round of the grog shops and taverns. Kidd stayed aboard, no doubt anxious to keep an eye on his share of the booty. Returning to the ship the crew brought back bad news: the *Adventure* had been listed as a pirate ship and her captain accused of armed robbery in areas under the jurisdiction of the Admiralty. Kidd still did not seem unduly worried. Even with the threat of imprisonment and a heavy fine, he was determined to return to New York and rely on his considerable influence to get him off.

John Somers (above) and the Duke of Shrewsbury (below), the backers who let Kidd down.

However, Kidd was well aware that the authorities in New York would obviously confiscate his treasure, so it is unthinkable that he did not hide it in a safe place, and what could have been easier than to bury his wealth among the twisting and winding creeks of Anguilla. On a dark night, with a light skiff, it would only have taken him an hour or so to glide into some jagged inlet, bury his chest of treasure deep in the sand and row back to the ship with no one the wiser. Not only would his treasure lie safe until happier times, but if the worst came to the worst, and he was condemned to a long imprisonment, he would have something to bargain with to regain his freedom. William Kidd still could not accept being branded a pirate. So, to this day, his gold and jewels must lie buried somewhere, maybe only a few kilometres from the town of Anguilla.

Kidd was so confident of his position, that when the *Quedagh Merchant* docked at Hispaniola, also in the West Indies and a safe port, he immediately took passage on the *Antonio* to New York. Oddly enough he still expected a good reception from his backers, especially when they learned the value of the cargo lying at Hispaniola. My Lords Bellemont, Somers, Romney and the Duke of Shrewsbury, much as they would have liked to have turned a blind eye, found themselves in a difficult position. Tales of Kidd's piracy, beyond doubt exaggerated, were the talk of the New World, so how could they protect a pirate? The fifth backer was Lord Oxford, First Lord of the Admiralty, and in no way was he prepared to jeopardize his position with the King of England, the overscrupulous William of Orange, for the sake of a sixth part of a cargo. Far from saving Kidd, the very importance of his aristocratic backers led to his undoing. Eager to dissociate themselves from what had become a piratical venture, they turned on Kidd, showering him with abuse, and the reluctant pirate was arrested and led in chains aboard an England-bound ship, to face charges of piracy on the high seas. He remained in prison for two years. Then, on 8 May 1701, he was brought to trial at the Old Bailey, and to his horror the three judges found him guilty and sentenced him to death, along with nine other members of his crew. Still protesting his innocence, he is supposed to have made the following proposal to his judges:

'I know where a prodigious treasure may be found. Spare my life and I shall tell you where it is.'

The judges were unimpressed. They had heard it all before, and Kidd's execution was fixed for 23 May 1701, at Execution Dock, where pirates and Navy offenders were hanged.

William Kidd's luck had run out with a vengeance. On the fateful morning he was led out and duly hanged, but the rope broke. As he lay gasping at the foot of the gallows, the prison chaplain, Paul Lorrain, extracted a confession from him. He confessed to piracy but not murder before he was hanged for a second time. This time there was no hitch. An unfortunate sea captain who casually drifted into piracy, he left behind a legend of swashbuckling bravado and bloodthirsty dealing that has been embroidered over the years in countless books and stories. Rumour and myth built his quite modest treasure into an immense fortune, a lure to a succession of treasure hunters.

Expedition after expedition set out in search of the pirate's hoard. At the end of the 19th century a claim was made that treasure to the value of £855 000 in gold had been found in Gardener's Island in the State of Maine, USA. This was supposedly Kidd's treasure, but it seems unlikely that Kidd would have risked burying it so close to home. One expedition sought the treasure in Nova Scotia, another in Nicaragua. Others searched Costa Rica, a number of places in the Far East and the Pacific Ocean. Many people searched around Madeira and the Canary Islands.

As late as 1950 a Canadian, Geoffrey Tayqui, sailed in an 80 ton cutter, *La Contenta*. On board was supposed to be a map marked by Kidd showing the exact position of the hoard. Nothing further was heard of this attempt. The flame was fanned again in 1953. Hubert Palmer, an English lawyer, bought weapons and chests which it was claimed had belonged to Captain Kidd. There, under the false bottom of one of the chests in best story book style lay part of a yellowed 18th century sea chart showing Skeleton Island. The top of the map was the coast of China. Sure enough, the other chests had false bottoms too, each containing a part of the chart which showed the exact location of Kidd's treasure on Skeleton Island. This information fitted nicely with the legend. Palmer died before he could finance an expedition but he willed the map, along with his other possessions, to his housekeeper. From her it found its way to a group of 13 adventurers. They sailed early one morning from Portsmouth, England, in a 120 ton schooner *La Morna*. Hardly out of port, they were hit by a violent storm and only managed to reach the Isle of Wight before they were hopelessly shipwrecked.

The Japanese then found some treasure. On an island south of the Japanese mainland, excavating archaeologists came across some piled silver bars and chests filled with gold. Immediately the cry went out: 'Kidd's Gold'.

Many people believe that William Kidd's treasure is still buried somewhere and the searches go on. But perhaps it was William Kidd himself who had the last word. He had recorded in his logs that most of his treasure had been lost at sea.

The Abominable Snowman

The fearsome creature stood erect, was tailless and covered in long hair.

On 8 November 1951, Eric Shipton, Michael Ward and Sherpa Tensing were returning from an Everest Reconnaissance Expedition. It was a clear day, but bitterly cold, as they began to cross the Menlung Glacier at about 5800 metres. There, sharply imprinted in the snow, were a line of footprints. They were man-like, but 46 centimetres long by 33 centimetres wide and the formation of four toes was clearly visible. Eric Shipton carefully photographed one of these prints, and the photograph was soon snapped up by the press. Could this at last be a footprint of a yeti, an abominable snowman? Overnight, the yeti became world news. Until Shipton's photograph was published in the newspapers, very few members of the public were aware of this elusive Himalayan legend. But is it a legend? Many experienced mountaineers and explorers are convinced that the yeti does exist, and the Nepalese take it for granted. Sightings have been few and brief as the creature, unlike the Loch Ness monster, has never allowed itself to be photographed, and only a handful of people have been able to give a detailed description of it.

Sceptics have offered a natural explanation for most sightings and photographs of footprints, but as yet no one has been able to explain away Shipton's photograph. Professor John Napier, a well-known anthropologist who has made a study of the yeti, says of the photograph:

'...as it stands, the footprint is not human, nor was it made by an ape or an ape-like creature known to science. What are the alternatives? No known creature anywhere in the world could leave such a spoor like this.... without it I would have no hesitation in dismissing the yeti as a red herring, or, at least, as a red bear. As it is the issue must lie on the table unresolved.'

John Hunt's base camp near Thyangboche Monastery, where he heard about a yeti.

What we know of the yeti comes mainly from the Sherpas, a mountain people inclined to mix fact with fantasy. They find it difficult to distinguish between the real world and the world of their religious beliefs. To them, the yeti is very real and mothers threaten their children with it when they are naughty, much as western mothers do with the 'bogeyman'. Sherpa Tensing, conqueror of Everest said at an interview:

'As Sherpas we are used to hearing from our childhood of stories about yeti from our older people, and even to this day [1955] you will find a naughty child hushed to silence when his mother says to him, "Hish, hish, here comes the yeti."'

Eric Shipton arrives at London Airport (above), his photographs safely in his briefcase. Later he presented his evidence of the existence of the yeti to the Royal Geographical Society. His famous photograph of a print (below) shows an impression of toes.

It is taboo for Sherpas to hunt or kill animals. In fact they take very little interest in them, and it is quite likely that they would mistake a yeti for a bear, langur monkey, or, for that matter, any other animal that roams the Himalayas. Their descriptions of the yeti range from miniature hairy men of various colours to massive four-metre-high giants. By sifting through their tales and selecting common data, we are able to build up a picture of this elusive creature.

The wide difference in size shows the existence of two types of yeti, the large nyalmo and the smaller, rimi. One investigator who has worked and travelled in the Himalayas for many, many years, claims that he has never met a Sherpa who has actually seen a yeti with his own eyes. It always appears that his brother, cousin or a friend has told him about it, and these relatives and friends never seem to be available.

Charles Wylie discussing the yeti with a yakherd. The Nepalese take the existence of the yeti for granted.

The picture of the yeti which emerges is that of a creature half man, half beast, varying in height from 1·5 metres to 4·5 metres. It is covered all over in a thick matting of hair, usually reddish-brown to dark brown or black in colour, with a lighter patch on the chest. It stoops slightly, and has heavy, hunched shoulders and long arms reaching below its knees.

The yeti walks partly on two legs and partly on all fours. Its face is mainly naked, often white-skinned, the features being more human than ape-like, and it has a thatch of long hair that falls over its deepset eyes. A muscular creature, it can uproot trees and lift and throw heavy boulders, and when on two legs it walks with a pigeon-toed gait. It lives either in caves high in the mountains, between 4000 and 6000 metres, or lower down in the impenetrable thickets and rhododendron forests of the lower slopes, around 3000 metres. A meat eater, it prowls at night in search of yaks and smaller mountain animals, but it has been known to raid villages and carry off human beings. Its high-pitched whistling call can be clearly heard over long distances, but it also roars and yelps. This is how the Sherpas see the yeti, a fearsome monster to be avoided at all costs.

When Lord Hunt (then John Hunt) visited the Thyangboche Monastery, the first base camp in his successful attempt on Everest, he heard an account of a yeti from the abbot. He writes:

'Seated with Charles Wylie and Tensing beside our host, a rotund figure robed in faded red, I questioned him about the yeti – better known to us as the abominable snowman. The dignitary at once warmed to this subject. Peering out of the window on to the meadow where our tents were pitched, he gave a most graphic description of how a yeti had appeared from the surrounding thickets, a few years back in the winter when the snow lay on the ground. This beast, loping along sometimes on its hind legs and sometimes on all fours, stood about five feet [1·5 metres] high and was covered with grey hair, a description which we have heard from other eye witnesses. Oblivious of his guests, the abbot was reliving a sight imprinted on his memory as he stared across at the scene of this event. The yeti had stopped to scratch – the old monk gave a good imitation, but went on longer than he need have done to make his point – had picked up snow, played with it and made a few grunts – again he gave us a convincing rendering. The inhabitants of the monastery had meanwhile worked themselves into a great state of excitement, and instructions were given to drive off the unwelcome visitor. Conch shells were blown and the long traditional horns sounded. The yeti had ambled away into the bush.'

Some Sherpa villages boast yeti scalps, which they hold sacred, but the ones that have been examined turned out to be the scalp hair of other animals. Two European investigators actually created a 'sacred yeti scalp' from goatskin. One folktale tells of a yeti that was captured by the villagers of the Jalap-La valley in north Sikkim. They placed a bucket of chang (a strong alcoholic drink,) in the yeti's path. It drank the chang and passed out. Quickly the villagers tied it up and carried it to their village. But as in all good folktales, the creature broke loose and escaped during the night.

Europeans as well as Sherpas have claimed to have seen mysterious man-like creatures in the Himalayan snows. These reports go back to the early 1800s. During the British Raj, many Indian Army officers and civil servants spent their leave game hunting and exploring in the Himalayas, often experiencing great hardship. The first recorded sighting of the yeti goes back to 1832 when one is mentioned in an article by B H Hodgson, British Resident at the court of Nepal. His native porters had rushed to him with a story of a wild man, a raksha or demon. They had been walking in a wood, when a wild man suddenly burst at them out of the bushes. The fearsome creature stood erect, was tailless and covered in long hair. One look at it and the natives fled in terror. Hodgson, who was convinced that they had seen an orang-utan, upbraided them for not shooting it.

Other reports began to appear in biographies and travel books. In 1889 in northern Sikkim, Major Waddell, an Indian Army officer, came across some mysterious tracks in the snow. Although a keen naturalist and a Fellow of the Linnaean Society, he was unable to identify the footprints as those of any known species of mammal. He was immediately told by his porters that the tracks were those of a yeti, but he was highly sceptical:

'On the most superficial investigation it always resolved into something that somebody had heard tell of. These so called hairy wild men are evidently the great yellow snow bears which are highly carnivorous and often kill yaks.'

Lieutenant-Colonel Howard-Bury, leader of the first Everest Reconnaissance Expedition in 1921, reported human-like footprints at about 6000 metres, but he also refused to accept them as those of a yeti, putting them down to '. . . . . . a large, loping grey wolf, which in the soft snow formed double tracks rather like those of a barefooted man.'

N A Tombazi.

People really began taking the existence of the yeti seriously in 1925, after an account by N A Tombazi, a photographer and Fellow of the Royal Geographical Society, hit the headlines. He was standing near the edge of his camp, at an altitude of 4500 metres, when one of his Sherpas started to shout and point. At first the intense glare and brightness of the snow prevented him from seeing anything, but after a few seconds, his eyes focused on a moving 'object', about 270 metres down the valley. He wrote:

'Unquestionably, the figure in outline was exactly like a human being, walking upright and stopping occasionally to uproot or pull up some dwarf rhododendron bushes. It showed up dark against the snow and as far as I could make out, wore no clothes. Within the next minute or so it had moved into some thick scrub and was lost to view.'

Unfortunately the creature had disappeared before Tombazi could take a photograph, but its footprints were still visible. They were about 15 centimetres long, 10 centimetres wide at the broadest part of the foot and they resembled the footprints of a man.

64

Frames from a film of 'Bigfoot', taken in 1967 at Bluff Creek, northern California, USA.

Probably the most sensational report of abominable snowmen came from Slavomir Rawicz, who, along with six of his friends, escaped from a Siberian prisoner of war camp in 1942. In his book, *The Long Walk*, he writes:

'The contours of the mountains hid them from view as we approached nearer, but when we halted on the edge of the bluff we found that they were still there, 12 feet or so [about 3·5 metres] below us and about 100 yards [90 metres] away. Two points struck me immediately. They were enormous and they walked on their hind legs. The picture is clear in my mind, fixed there indelibly by a solid two hours of observation. We could just not believe what we saw at first, so we stayed to watch . . . I set myself to estimate their height on the basis of my military training for artillery observations. They could not have been much less than eight feet [2·5 metres] tall. One was a few inches taller than the other, in the relation of the average man to the average woman. They were shuffling quietly round on a flattish shelf which formed part of the obvious route for us to continue our descent. We thought that if we waited long enough they would go away and leave the way clear for us. It was obvious they had seen us, and it was equally apparent they had no fear of us. The American said that eventually he was sure we would see them drop on all fours like bears. But they never did. Their faces I could not see in detail, but the heads were squarish and the ears must lie close to the skull because there was no projection from the silhouette against the snow. The shoulders sloped sharply down to a powerful chest. The arms were long and the wrists reached the level of the knees. Seen in profile, the back of the head was a straight line from the crown into the shoulders, ''like a damned Prussian,'' as P put it. We decided unanimously that we were examining a type of creature of which we had no previous experience in the wild, in zoos or in literature. It would have been easy to have seen them waddle off at a distance and dismissed them as either bear or big ape of the orang-utang species. At close range they defied facile description. There was something both of the bear and ape about their general shape, but they could not be mistaken for either. The colour was a rusty kind of brown. They appeared to be covered by two distinct kinds of hair – the reddish brown which gave them their characteristic colour forming a tight, close fur against the body, mingling with which were long, loose, straight hairs, hanging downwards, which had a slight greyish tinge as the light caught them. . . . . Their heads turned towards us now and again, but their interest in us seemed to be of the slightest. . . What were they? For years they remained a mystery to me, but since recently I have read of scientific expeditions to discover the abominable snowman of the Himalayas and studied descriptions of the creature given by native hillmen, I believe that on that day we may have encountered two of the animals. I do insist however, that recent estimates of their height as about five feet [1·5 metres] must be wrong. The minimum height of a well-grown specimen must be around seven feet [2 metres].

During the 1950s, reports came in from mountaineers and members of the *London Daily Express* expeditions of 1954 and 1957. There were no confirmed sightings, but a number of photographs were taken, but none that could not be explained. The most recent account by a Russian expedition claims to have photographed footprints that could only have been made by a man-like creature.

But doubt surrounds the various reported sightings and photographs, by both Sherpas and Europeans. Over-large footprints have been accounted for by the melting action of the sun. Many reported sightings could have been langur monkeys, which are large, able to stand on two legs and have been seen at heights of up to 3500 metres.

But we are left with Eric Shipton's photograph. The footprint is sharp and clear, the outline unaffected by melting. No one has accounted for it and it still remains a complete mystery. Perhaps someone will soon provide proof of what sort of creature made that print.

No one has proved the existence of an abominable snowman, but people claim they have evidence of huge man-like creatures from many different countries. Shown here are the tracks found by Eric Shipton on the Menlung Glacier (top left), a track of 'Bigfoot' from America (bottom left), a sculpture of the creature (top right) and a cast of a track found in Russia (bottom right).

The Derelict

The vessel had been sailing herself, driven remorselessly towards land by a blustering westerly wind.

The old sailing ship creaked and groaned as she buffeted her way through the squally mid-winter sea. The *Dei Gratia*, from New York bound for Gibraltar, was still almost 1000 kilometres from her destination – 1000 kilometres of dreary, grey Atlantic. It was 5 December, 1872 and the ship's master, Captain David Morehouse was on watch. Off watch below the first mate, Oliver Deveau, a Canadian, heard the captain shout so he lurched up the companionway to the heaving deck.

'Sail on the windward bow. Seems to be in distress Mr Deveau.'

Through his glass the mate could make out the grey shadow of another sailing ship. She appeared to be about 8 kilometres off.

Dimly he could see a tattered Stars and Stripes fluttering in the wind while the vessel yawed and pitched in the heavy sea. She looked to be a half-brig of about 300 tons and 30 metres long. Only two of her sails were set. The others were either torn to rags or furled. She was aimlessly driving forward at the mercy of the wind. As the *Dei Gratia* closed up, the name on the stern of the mystery ship came into focus – *Mary Celeste*. One of the most baffling mysteries of the sea was about to unfold.

'Brig ahoy! Brig ahoy!' the captain hailed the other vessel through his speaking trumpet.

No answer.

'Seems to be deserted, better take a couple of hands and go aboard, Mr Deveau,' said the captain, his mind on possible salvage money. A boat was launched, and Deveau, John Wright the second mate, and one of the hands pulled towards the *Mary Celeste*. Alongside, they hailed her again but there was still no answer. It was no easy task for Deveau and Wright to clamber aboard as the ship lurched drunkenly through the water, but within minutes they were standing on the deserted deck. Nervously they looked about them at the eerie scene.

The *Mary Celeste* had shipped a lot of water and appeared to be leaking badly. Water was slopping over the sill of the galley door. Deveau made his way below from the deckhouse, fearful of what he might find. Wright had already hinted at the possibility of Yellow Jack, that terrible fever that could wipe out a whole crew. Nothing! The cabins were empty. Lying on the table of the saloon, the log slate showed an entry for 25 November, 10 days ago. That could mean that the vessel had been sailing herself since then, driven remorselessly towards land by a blustering westerly wind. In the captain's cabin a melodeon with a sheet of music on it stood against the partition dividing the cabin from the saloon. There was a sewing machine on a small desk alongside some women's clothing and a child's toy. These must have belonged to the captain's wife and small daughter. Washing was hung out in the crew's quarters and everything was shipshape, with the crew's belongings and sea chests neatly stowed away. For whatever reason they had left, the crew had left in a hurry. What horror had forced an entire crew to abandon their ship and take to an open boat in the middle of an Atlantic winter?

Meanwhile, Wright had discovered that the brig had only shipped 1 metre of water; a couple of hours work and she could be pumped dry. In the hold was a cargo of alcohol – one barrel broached – stores for six months and plenty of fresh water. Why had the ship been abandoned? Everything seemed to be in place, no signs of a struggle, no signs of being smashed by heavy seas – a bottle of oil for the sewing machine and a reel of cotton both stood upright on a narrow shelf. The mystery deepened.

'What do you think?'

Deveau looked round the ship and nodded. He knew what Wright meant, it would mean a pretty penny to the crew of the *Dei Gratia* in salvage money if they could sail her the 1000 kilometres to Gibraltar. The captain agreed when this suggestion was put to him. He too, could do with the salvage money.

Captain David Morehouse, master of the Dei Gratia. *It was hinted that he was involved in a scheme to defraud the insurance company.*

Deveau and only two others sailed the *Mary Celeste* to the port at the entrance to the Mediterranean, no mean feat of seamanship. They arrived only 24 hours after the *Dei Gratia*. Any expectation of a warm welcome was soon dispelled. Going aboard the *Dei Gratia*, Deveau was informed that the harbour authorities were deeply suspicious and intended to hold a detailed enquiry. The customary notice of arrest was nailed to the main mast of the *Mary Celeste*, and ugly rumours began to fly around the 'Rock'. Captain Morehouse speedily sent a cablegram to the brokers in New York – 'FOUND FOURTH AND BROUGHT HERE MARY CELESTE ABANDONED SEAWORTHY ADMIRALTY IMPOST NOTIFY ALL PARTIES TELEGRAPH OFFER OF SALVAGE.' The answer came and the *Dei Gratia* was free to proceed to Genoa with her cargo of petroleum. Captain Morehouse was promised up to half the salvage money of $17 400 on the *Mary Celeste* and half the value of the cargo insured in sterling, thought to be £6522. 3s. 0d. (£6522.15p). A nice haul for penniless sailors. It would seem that the affair would be rapidly resolved.

However, nobody had reckoned with Solly Flood, a belligerent and ambitious Irishman. In his position as Advocate and Proctor for the Queen in the Office of the Admiralty, he was determined to ferret and probe, so squeezing the maximum amount of glory out of the situation. There was also an added complication. On the same day as Morehouse had sent his cable, the American Consul in Gibraltar, Horatio J Sprague, had telegraphed the Board of Underwriters in New York: 'BRIG MARY CELESTE HERE DERELICT IMPORTANT SEND POWER ATTORNEY TO CLAIM HER FROM ADMIRALTY COURT.' The affair was building up to an international incident and the hopes of Captain Morehouse for a rapid settlement began to recede.

Captain Benjamin Spooner Briggs.

The Enquiry opened in Gibraltar in mid-December 1872. The *Mary Celeste* had sailed from New York with a cargo of alcohol. Her master, Captain Benjamin Spooner Briggs had taken his wife and two-year old daughter, Sophia, along with him on the voyage. They had totally disappeared together with the crew. The thinly-veiled sarcasm of Solly Flood as, resplendent in wig and gown he cross-examined the witnesses, made it only too obvious that he believed the evidence being given by the crew of the *Dei Gratia* to be untrue. The simple sailors, no match for a professional barrister, did not appear in a very good light. He asked for an adjournment and the court adjourned.

Flood, together with four naval captains and a Colonel of Engineers, went aboard the *Mary Celeste* and began a thorough examination. The navy men were inclined to believe that the brig had been battered in heavy weather, but Flood had other ideas. Fussing round the cabins he dived under the captain's bunk and triumphantly held up an old sword. It was one of Italian make which Captain Briggs had picked up as a souvenir when visiting an old battlefield near the head of the Adriatic on a previous voyage. Drawing it from its scabbard, Solly Flood pointed to rusty marks on the blade. They had to be blood. He then discovered the barrel of alcohol which had been broached, and a scar in the wood of the handrail further heated his imagination. By the end of the examination he had a theory.

He was convinced that the crew had got at the alcohol, and in a fit of drunken frenzy murdered the captain, his wife and daughter and the first mate. Sometime between 25 November and 5 December the crew were then taken aboard some vessel bound for the West Indies or some North or South American port. (It is hard to believe that just any ship would pick up a captain-less crew in such circumstances.) The two deep scores running each side of the ship from the bows, both about 1 centimetre deep and about 2 metres long, were, according to Flood, made by the mutineers to give the impression that the ship was unseaworthy.

After three months, the sensational developments which people were expecting did not arise. The Admiralty Court in effect returned an open verdict upon the incident and the master and crew of the *Dei Gratia* were reluctantly granted £1700 in salvage awards – a fraction of the amount that they considered their due.

The American authorities were up in arms. In their eyes the British were casting discredit, without a fragment of evidence, on the American maritime marine. Theories flowed in from the other side of the Atlantic. One story appearing in the *New York Sun* immediately after the Enquiry was headed: 'The Abandoned Ship – No Mutiny but a Scheme to Defraud the Insurance Company.' The suggestion was that Captain Briggs had entered into a plot with another vessel to stage a fake abandonment with the object of collecting salvage money. By implication this pointed a finger at the *Dei Gratia*. Doubt was cast on the evidence of the captain and crew of that ship. How was it that they didn't identify the brig until they actually boarded her?

Towards the end of the Enquiry in Gibraltar, it had been murmured that perhaps Captain Morehouse had not been quite open with the court. It was not until 1927 that evidence was brought forward to show that in actual fact Captain Morehouse and Captain Briggs had been firm friends of several years standing, and before the *Mary Celeste* sailed from New York they had dined together. In 1956 an American historian went even further. He said:

'It is also known that the brigantine *Dei Gratia* of Nova Scotian registry, was in New York loading cargo while the *Celeste* prepared for her voyage into history. Skipper Briggs and Skipper Morehouse were old friends; they had encountered each other in many of the ports of the seven seas. Morehouse, like Briggs, was part-owner and master of his ship, and sometimes took his wife along on his cruises. Mrs Briggs and Mrs Morehouse, like their husbands, were also good friends and had met at ports-of-call in various parts of the world.'

Yet not a word of this came out at the Enquiry. Is it possible that Morehouse, following hard on the heels of the *Mary Celeste* could have failed to recognize her, even on a grey day, when he discovered the derelict vessel?

Months then years went by and there was not a sign of any of the Briggs family, or the crew. The doubts arising from the Enquiry grew rather than lessened over the years and the legend of the 'Ghost Ship', *Mary Celeste*, was blown up into a major mystery. Theory after theory was put forward, and for one reason or another each was discarded. Sir Arthur Conan Doyle, ever one for a mystery, whether fairy photographs or paranormal phenomena, wrote a short story which he claimed solved the enigma of the American brig. Then came a 'revelation' in the *Strand Magazine* of October 1913 – 'Amazing Solution of the Mystery of *Marie Celeste*.' (Conan Doyle had seen fit in his story to change the original Mary to Marie.)

Mr Howard Linford MA, headmaster of a Hampstead preparatory school had discovered a manuscript among the effects of an elderly school servant who had died. In the manuscript, the servant, Abel Fosdyk, claimed to have been steward aboard the *Mary Celeste*. No one could doubt the word of the headmaster so they thought that this must be the true version. The editor of the *Strand Magazine* described the story as 'so vivid and so alive, so simple and yet so unlikely to be thought of, that one seems to hear the ring of truth in every word.'

Fosdyk's manuscript claimed that Captain Briggs had gone stark staring mad. Despite battling against a roaring gale the captain refused to leave the wheel, hanging from the spokes, almost dead to the world, his eyes wild with madness. A man fell overboard from the yards, so the captain ordered his first mate to jump, fully clothed, into the seething cauldron of sea to rescue him. The mate naturally refused and Briggs accused him of cowardice and said that everyone on board was a coward. The crew managed, with the aid of his wife, to get the captain below and tucked in his bunk. His wife, poor woman, was only too aware of his condition.

Later, while the gale continued to rage, the captain's daughter, a sturdy, square-built girl with short reddish hair, and according to Fosdyk, seven or eight years old, walked out on to the bowsprit of the ship. Fosdyk rescued her and reported the incident to Briggs, who ordered the carpenter to build a 'quarter deck' for 'Baby' – an upturned table with a rail, lashed to the bowsprit.

Mrs Briggs and her son, Arthur.

Next day the crazy captain was determined to swim around the ship fully-clothed, to prove that at least one man aboard the *Mary Celeste* was not a coward. Two men, stripped to their pants, offered to accompany him. The storm had abated and the sea was flat calm. The three men jumped in and began swimming. The crew with Mrs Briggs and Baby stood on 'Baby's quarter deck' to watch. As they all moved to the port side, the 'quarter deck' collapsed and they were thrown into the water – all except one man left hanging to the platform which was dangling from the bowsprit. Abel Fosdyk surfaced and swam towards the survivor, grabbing at the platform which, with his extra weight, collapsed into the sea. Someone shrieked, 'There's a shark after us.' A fin cut through the water and Briggs who had still been swimming round, disappeared screaming. Clinging to 'Baby's quarter deck', Fosdyk, the sole survivor, watched the *Mary Celeste* sail away into the distance.

An unlikely story, yet the *Strand Magazine* claimed it to be authentic, at a time when it was at the height of its influence, with a large international circulation.

In many ways the *Mary Celeste* was unsinkable. In their issue of 24 September 1924, London's *Daily Express* carried the headline:

'Great Sea Mystery Cleared Up.
Derelict Gold: Crew's Escape with Stolen £3500.'

Captain Lucy was retired, and, at the age of 70, claimed to be the only man alive who knew the truth of the matter. He had heard the true story when mate of the *Island Princess* in the South Seas from a man called Triggs who told him that he used to be bosun on the ill-fated *Mary Celeste*. Naturally it was told under oath, and now, Triggs being long dead, Captain Lucy felt at liberty to reveal the truth – for a fee.

In this version Captain Briggs was the villain. The *Mary Celeste* ran in with a derelict steamer, the boarding party found £3500 in gold and silver coin, and after opening the steamer's seacocks – at the captain's instruction – the crew divided the money between them. Briggs had £1200 for his share, the mate £600, and second mate £400, Triggs, the bosun, £300 and the remainder was equally divided among the crew. Then Briggs and his men abandoned the *Mary Celeste* and headed for Cadiz in the ship's boats. This story fails to explain why Briggs should suggest abandoning the brig, of which he was part-owner, for a sum far less than his share of the ship was worth, not counting a cargo worth more than £6000.

Then in 1929 came Keating's hoax. He wrote a book about John Pemberton, a 92-year old, who was apparently a survivor from the *Mary Celeste* now living in Liverpool. Later, Pemberton's story by 'Our special correspondent', appeared in the London *Evening Standard* under the title, 'A Tale that Joseph Conrad Might Have Written'. It was printed together with a photograph and once again *this* was the true solution! In this story Briggs was in New York without a crew, and Morehouse was there without a cargo. Briggs offered Morehouse half the cargo if he would share his crew and a bargain was struck. The mate of the *Mary Celeste*, Hullock, took over the ship when Briggs lost his senses after the death of his wife in a storm. Briggs fell overboard while unconscious and another member of the crew followed him during a fight. The mate and the crew members who were not originally from the *Dei Gratia*, fearing that they would be had up for murder, left the *Mary Celeste* in one of the boats. The *Dei Gratia* crew decided to return to their own ship and Pemberton insisted on staying behind as well. Days later, the *Mary Celeste* happened to come across the *Dei Gratia* at sea and so it was that the two ships were manned only by the crew of the *Dei Gratia*. Pemberton kept quiet, afraid of being arrested for murder and returned to Liverpool.

Many years later, it was discovered that the 'special correspondent' was in fact Laurence Keating and the photograph, a picture of Keating's own father. Pemberton had never existed.

Despite the unlikely solutions put forward, the mystery still remains. What did happen that fateful December day aboard the *Mary Celeste*?

Mysterious Footprints

As the day wore on, news came of other parishes that had been visited by the mysterious hoofed creature.

George Fairly, trudging through the snowy streets of Topsham in south Devonshire in the early morning light of 9 February 1855, could not remember ever having been so cold. It was the worst winter in living memory, and the previous night a sudden severe frost had frozen over the rivers, trapping birds where they stood in the ice. The thick carpet of snow lay unbroken in the deserted streets. 'Who'd be a baker,' George thought to himself, 'up on a morning like this, while other folk are warm and snug in their beds?'

Suddenly he pulled up with a jerk. Someone *had* been about. A line of footprints led up the street, exceptionally clearly defined, as if they had been burned in the snow. Peering more closely he realized that these were very unusual prints indeed. 10 centimetres long, 6 centimetres wide and 20 centimetres apart, they appeared to have been made by a hoofed creature walking upright on two legs. But curiously, the hoofmarks, footprints or whatever they were, were regularly spaced one behind the other in a single row. It was as if the creature who had made them had put one foot delicately, and exactly centrally, in front of the other. Puzzled, George followed the tracks which were going in the general direction of his bakery. A metre short of his shop door, the strange marks turned abruptly right, and followed the high brick wall of his bakery yard for a few metres. There they stopped short at the base of the wall. Whatever had made the marks had simply vanished.

Intrigued, George searched around for fur-

ther signs of his early morning visitor. The snow, where it curved over the top of the wall, had been disturbed directly above the last mark and sure enough, the tracks continued along the top of the wall in a dead straight line. Whatever the creature was it must have leaped up, landed without scuffling the snow and then picked its way along the narrow single row of bricks to the end of the wall. Here the little hoof-like marks again took to the ground, trailing across a field leading to the estuary of the River Exe. George was curious, but not sufficiently curious to follow the tracks any further. It was bitterly cold and his warm ovens were calling him.

His early customers began to come in, full of tales of the mysterious hoofprints that were apparently all around the town. By mid-morning the rumours were flying thick and fast, as each customer had something fresh to relate. The mysterious prints had been found in the most inaccessible places – up the sides of walls, across housetops, in gardens and courtyards enclosed by high walls and palings – as well as in open spaces. As the day wore on news came of other parishes that had been visited by the mysterious hoofed creature. Gradually a pattern began to emerge. After it had stopped snowing at about 11 o'clock, a strange being had crossed the countryside leaving a single line of mincing tracks, travelling from village to village for over 160 kilometres. These tracks followed a trail from Exmouth on the coast, north through Raliegh and Bicton, then turned west to Woodbury, through Topsham and across the fields to the banks of the Exe. At the water's edge the tracks stopped, only to appear again on the opposite bank at Powderham, 3 kilometres away. Nothing impeded their progress or disturbed their even spacing of 30 centimetres, as they meandered to Luscombe,

Dawlish and Teignmouth. There at the bank of the River Teign, the tracks again vanished, to reappear on the south shore at Newton, several kilometres away. Then on to Torquay and from there across the snowy fields of Totnes. There is no evidence that the tracks went beyond there.

What sort of creature could cover over 160 kilometres in a single night, prancing across open fields, through or over freezing water, leaving thousands of hoofprints in an unbroken line? What was this thing that could walk up vertical walls, cross housetops, crawl through narrow drains and walk straight through haystacks? Where did it come from and where did it vanish to? By nightfall, gossip had credited the creature with supernatural powers. The cloven hooves could mean only one thing – the Devil! Panic swept the area and in country districts villagers locked themselves in their cottages refusing to go out after sunset. Fireside gossip had it that the Devil had walked across Devon and the villagers were taking no chances.

The clergy did their best to calm down their parishioners. One vicar, the Reverend Henry Fudsen, gave a sermon in which he maintained that the prints were the paw marks of several cats. But the local people who had seen the hoofprints for themselves knew better.

Hundreds of accounts poured into the newspaper offices, accounts that seemed to have no rational explanation. One group of industrious trackers followed the hoofprints to a haystack. The 'creature' had apparently gone straight through the haystack instead of over the top, as in most cases. The prints simply stopped at one side and then continued on the other. Later the trackers came upon a set of prints which led over the roofs of about six houses. In one village the tracks led into a shed and out of the other side. Whatever had made them had gone through a hole only 15 centimetres wide. In another village the mysterious being appeared to have crawled through a drainpipe, leaving tracks at both ends. Near the village of Dawlish, the trail led into dense bracken and undergrowth. Thinking to have tracked the creature to its lair, the locals attempted to flush it out with dogs, but the dogs would have none of it. Bursting from the thicket they dashed off, howling piteously. No wonder the superstitious 19th-century folk believed the hoofprints to be supernatural. Nevertheless, a number of hardy souls plucked up courage and decided to hunt down the night prowler. In bands armed with fowling pieces, pitchforks and sickles, they set out to comb the area, but without success.

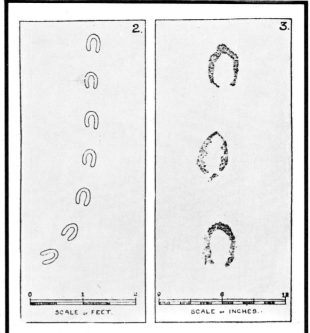

These drawings of the footprints, by local eyewitnesses, appeared in newspapers to illustrate accounts of the mysterious visitor.

The Times newspaper sent a reporter down to Devon to sift the evidence and printed its first article under the heading 'Extraordinary Circumstances', a week after the event. With its usual calm assurance *The Times* stated that there had been great excitement in parts of Devon, where some strange creature of remarkable powers had left footprints in the snow on rooftops, walls and in courtyards enclosed by high walls. It further continued:

'The track appeared more like that of a biped than a quadruped, and the steps were generally eight inches [20 centimetres] in advance of each other. The impressions of feet closely resembled those of a donkey's shoe, and measured from an inch and a half to (in some instances) two and a half inches across [about 4 – 6 centimetres]. Here and there it appeared as if cloven, but in the generality of the steps the shoe was continuous, and from the snow in the 'centre remaining entire, merely showing the outer crest of the foot, it must have been concave.'

There was certainly no lack of theories to account for the strange happenings, but none of them came anywhere near to solving the mystery. The tracks of all likely birds and animals were minutely examined and compared with the singular hoofprints, and a fine crop of answers was put forward. The favourite choices of the bird fanciers were seagulls, cranes, swans, turkeys and moorhens. Animal fanciers favoured foxes, otters, hares, rabbits, and even toads. One investigator, in all seriousness, suggested a donkey or pony with a broken shoe. Could a pony cover that distance in five hours, taking walls and roofs in its stride?

The Reverend G M Musgrave was among the first to account for the mystery. He calmly informed his nervous parishioners that the footprints had been made by nothing more mysterious than a kangaroo. A kangaroo can jump – but on to a roof? And, what was a kangaroo doing roaming the Devon countryside? That it 'had escaped from a travelling menagerie, then returned to its cage without anyone noticing its absence is, to say the least, highly unlikely.

A certain Tom Fox was convinced that the prints were that of a jumping rat which had the ability to land on all four feet together. A nice suggestion was that the marks had been caused by a rope trailing from a balloon. When approached, the British Museum and the Zoological Society poured scorn on all these notions, but they themselves were unable to offer any alternative suggestions.

One on-the-spot investigator put the situation into a nutshell when he said:

'No known animal could have traversed this extent of country in one night, besides having crossed an estuary 2 miles broad [about 3 kilometres]. Neither does any known animal walk in a line of single footsteps . . . birds could not have left these marks as no bird's foot leaves the impression of a hoof.'

Then Professor Richard Owen, a famous naturalist, weighed in with his considered verdict – badgers! As he pointed out, a badger's paw makes a print bigger than itself. A badger also carefully places its hind paws in the same place as its forepaws. He did admit however, that one badger could not have covered the distance, much less swum the estuary. But undismayed, he went on to point out that there would be many hungry badgers about on such a night, and what seemed to be the tracks of one animal were in fact the tracks of many animals. It was with a fine unconcern that he totally disregarded the problems that would face the average badger climbing the vertical wall of a house, leaping high walls or walking straight through a haystack. The country folk of Devon knew better – it was the Devil. Did not one investigator, all the way from London, say that the prints were so clearly defined that they looked as though they had been burned in the snow by a hot iron? Old Nick's cloven hooves would have been pretty hot coming straight from Hell.

But Devon was by no means the only place to receive a visitation from 'the Pit'. A German from Heidleberg, on hearing of the Devon prints, wrote to the *Illustrated London News* in the following March, pointing out that similar tracks could be seen every year in sand and snow on a hill on the Polish border.

One of the most recent theories of the Devon visitation, is that the prints were made by an unknown arctic bird driven south by a particularly cold and savage winter in search of food. This seems just as likely as badgers, jumping rats, kangaroos or the Devil.

Professor Richard Owen.

The Search for Gold

Even the fountains, water pipes and courtyard statues were made of pure gold.

When Hernán Cortés arrived back in Spain in 1520, he brought with him, from the rich city of Tenochtitlan in Mexico, stories of treasure beyond the wildest dreams of Europeans. Montezuma, the all-powerful ruler, had laden him with priceless gifts. 'A disc in the shape of the sun, as big as a cartwheel and made of a very fine gold, another large disc of brightly shining silver in the shape of a moon . . . . . 20 golden ducks of fine workmanship, some ornaments in the shape of their dogs, many others in the shape of tigers, lions and monkeys.' The inventory went on and on. Cortés had discovered a land across the Western Sea, whose very mountains seemed to be made of gold – gold, that irresistable lure to a European. Soon gold fever ran through the Spanish court, and nobles and adventurers rubbed shoulders in the antechambers waiting to plead their cause with the king.

Perched high in a tree, the Aztec lookout in this old print, sights Cortés's ship.

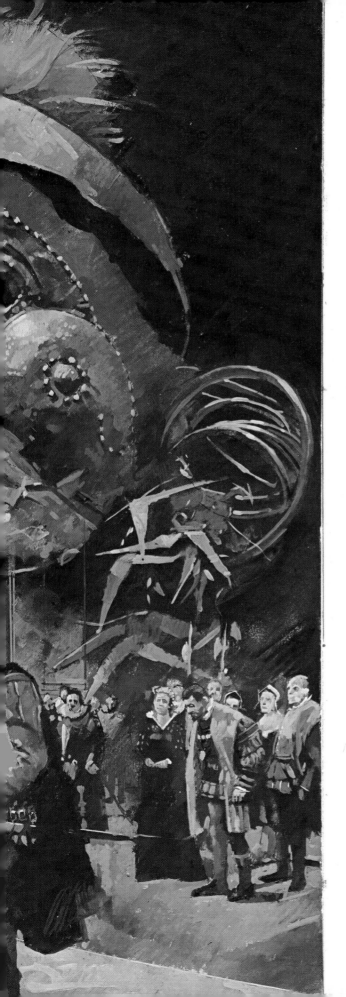

Above: How the Mexicans of the day saw Hernán Cortés and his fearful horses.
Below: Francisco Pizarro.

General Francisco Pizarro was the adventurer chosen by the Spanish king, Charles I, to bring back a fortune to Spain. In 1531 Pizarro, together with a handful of horses and 185 foot soldiers, set sail for the New World. After a short stop in Panama to season his raw recruits for battle, he sailed south to Peru, arriving some weeks later at the northern frontier of the Inca Empire.

The Incas had a vast empire, on the west coast of South America, that reached its peak in the 14th century. They built elaborate cities, not only along the Pacific coast but in the high, remote Andes, and even in the impenetrable forests of the Amazon Basin. The empire had two capitals, Quitu in the north (now Quito, capital of Ecuador), and Cuzco, further south in Peru. These capitals, as well as the other Inca towns, were joined by a network of great roads across snow-covered mountains and through valleys. Galleries were cut through solid rock, bridges were suspended over rivers, and cliffs scaled by stairways. The ruler, known as the Inca, lived in his southern capital of Cuzco, and when he died, his body was embalmed, dressed in a suit of gold and seated in the temple of his ancestors. All his temples, with one exception, were closed, and all his treasures were shut away for ever, just as he had left them. His successor had to provide himself with new temples and treasures.

Atahualpa, Inca of Peru, murdered by Francisco Pizarro.

The Incas, believing that they were all children of the Sun, valued gold only because it was a symbol of the Sun. To them it had no monetary value, but was merely a religious symbol used for making life-size idols and other religious objects. The lords ate from golden plates and drank from cups of precious metal. Even the fountains, water pipes and courtyard statues were made of pure gold. As if it was a gift from the Sun, the gold was brought to the Incas, in enormous quantities, by the rivers which washed it down from the peaks of the Andes. No wonder that the avaricious Pizarro was eager to push south into the Empire of Gold.

The ruler, or Inca, was considered to be a descendant of the Sun God, and was himself worshipped as a god. His word was absolute law and he lived in breathtaking splendour. His palaces and temples were roofed with slabs of solid gold that sparkled in the sun.

Runners brought the news of the arrival of Pizarro to Atahualpa, Son of the Sun and present Inca. From his palace he sent a delegation of high priests and lesser members of his family to greet the Spaniard and offer him, as a token of friendship, seven priceless emeralds and an array of gold objects. Realizing that the stories he had heard were true, Pizarro broke camp and with his men and horses, headed south to meet Atahualpa. If he could conquer the country peacefully, so much the better, if not, he and his men were prepared to fight to the death for such a golden prize.

Sweating and struggling in the great heat, the conquistadores still refused to remove their iron helmets and breastplates, and were always on the look-out for attack. As they marched into the interior unopposed, messengers were sent ahead to inform Atahualpa that the Spaniards were coming in friendship. After six days marching over mighty mountains and tremendous gorges, and hacking a way through rain forests, Pizarro entered a fertile valley. There lay the city of Caxamalca, its gold roofs gleaming in the sun.

Later in the afternoon Pizarro and his little band of men, trailing their pikes and muskets, straggled into the great square in front of the Inca's palace. There, drawn up on three sides of the square, were row upon row of Inca warriors. There were tens of thousands of picked troops armed with bronze-tipped spears and bows and arrows. Pizarro and his men, numb with shock, could only gaze in horror at this vast horde. Deciding to brazen it out, Pizarro spurred his horse forward and his little band followed. An excited murmur ran through the ranks of the assembled soldiers, many of whom fell to their knees in worship. It was the horses.

The superstitious Indians had never seen horses before and immediately took them for minor gods. Heartened by this, Pizarro pitched his tents in full view of the Inca army, and conferred with his officers. Between them they hit upon a bold plan. They would seize Atahualpa and hold him as hostage.

On the following day, Atahualpa arrived borne on the shoulders of his generals in a gold litter encrusted with rubies, emeralds and other precious stones. The officials surrounding him 'blazed like the sun', so wrote one of the Spaniards. The Inca wore a magnificent ankle-length robe fashioned from pure gold. A plumed headdress was held in place by a crown of gold in the centre of which blazed an enormous emerald. From his arms hung jewelled bracelets, and a pair of finely wrought gold earrings reached almost to his shoulders. Around his neck he wore a collar of emeralds. There was absolute silence in the square as he stepped from his litter and walked towards the seemingly unarmed Spaniards. His own troops had already grounded their weapons as a sign of friendship.

Pizarro stepped forward and with a fine show of arrogance declared in a loud voice, 'I come as the Ambassador of the King of Spain, the most powerful monarch of the world, to bring this country to subjugation to its rightful lord, to snatch it from the darkness of barbarism, and to convert it to the only true religion of Jesus Christ.' Whereupon, he dropped a white handkerchief and the Spaniards threw off their cloaks and, led by the fearful horses, they dashed forward with their hidden weapons. A volley of musket fire laid low the officials surrounding the Inca. His troops, terrified of the horses and musket fire, offered no resistance, and over 3000 of them were slaughtered where they stood. Atahualpa was seized and the pillaging began. The palace was sacked and a vast treasure taken, but this was trivial compared with the ransom offered by the Inca for his freedom.

Atahualpa was imprisoned in a cell measuring, according to Francisco de Xeres, Pizarro's secretary, 17 by 22 feet (5 by 7 metres). A line was drawn round the cell about 3 metres from the ground, and the room was to be filled up to this line with gold. That was the extent of the Inca's ransom, representing over 400 000 kilograms of gold. The time agreed for delivery of the ransom was two months. Soon, glittering piles of gold were flooding in from all parts of the empire. Although the Incas were keeping their part of the bargain, Pizarro realized that he could not afford to free Atahualpa at any price. He could still muster enormous reserves

A European engraving of the fortified city of Cuzco, capital of the Peruvian Incas, children of the Sun.

of troops who would not be tricked a second time. So the Inca was sentenced to death. To ease his conscience, Pizarro put about the false story that Atahualpa had tried to stir up an insurrection. After he was baptized, to assure that he would die a Christian, Atahualpa was led out into the square and killed in front of thousands of his followers. But while awaiting his execution, it is thought that Atahualpa had secretly sent out an order to his high priests instructing them to dismantle the gold from the sacred temples and bury it, along with the idols and other treasures, to keep them from falling into the hands of the greedy Spaniards.

When the news of the murder reached the Incas, the flow of gold into Caxamalca ceased. Much of it was buried in forests and caves, some was thrown into the lakes and rivers. Priests removed tonnes of treasure from the Temple of the Virgins of the Sun, including huge blocks of solid gold and chests of emeralds. These they lowered into a deep gorge on the precipitous slopes of a volcano, home of the Fire God. The treasure supposedly hidden throughout the empire gave rise to stories and legends. Some possibly are true, but others are obviously fantasy, built up as more and more people went in search of the treasure.

The Spaniards, led by the fearful horses, dashed forward with their hidden weapons.

One of the more likely stories concerns the treasure thrown into Lake Titicaca. This lake is over 190 kilometres long, and lies at 3918 metres above sea level, between Peru and Bolivia. It was on an island in Titicaca that the Incas thought that Manco Capac was created first Inca by the Sun God, and from that day the island became the centre of pilgrimage. At least once in a lifetime, each Inca was supposed to make a pilgrimage to Titicaca bearing a gift of precious metal. Garcilaso de la Vega wrote:

'The Indians built a resplendent temple there, with walls covered in gold leaf. Each year the provinces of the Empire sent up offerings of considerable value in the form of gold and silver, to give thanks to the Sun God.'

It is said that the priests stripped the temple, and, rowing out to the middle of the lake dropped the treasure into the murky waters, where it sank to the bottom, over 180 metres below. Over the centuries many plans have been made to recover the gold, but at a height of 3918 metres, free divers can only operate at a depth of 18 metres owing to the pressure. There have been ambitious schemes to drain the lake but they have proved too costly. After all, there may not be any treasure there.

When reports of the gold that Pizarro and his followers had found were heard, people became very interested in the already known legend of El Dorado. It was a German, Ambrosius Dalfinger, who, in 1529, had first set out to find El Dorado, the Golden Man. Charles I of Spain had given his German bankers governorship of

The Indians valued gold less than did their Spanish conquerors.

Dalfinger's party was attacked by Indians.

Venezuela, as a surety for a loan. The Germans despatched young Dalfinger to act as governor of Venezuela. Immediately, he set off into the interior with 180 men to explore the possibilities of his domain. At Lake Maracaibo he heard the legend of El Dorado. Deep in the interior there lived a people with whom local Indians traded; a people who covered their temple and houses with gold; a people who used gold as a base metal. At the edge of a sacred lake called Guatavita was the town of a great ruler, El Dorado, the Gilded Man. In the centre of the town was a temple full of gold idols, and their eyes were emeralds. At sunset each day the wives of the chieftain anointed his body with sap from trees, and covered it with a thick layer of gold dust. At the sinking of the sun he dived into the water of the sacred lake to wash away the gold. Afterwards the high priests threw gold bars and handfuls of emeralds into the lake.

Dalfinger, fired by the legend, pushed on, but his already depleted party was attacked by Indians. He died from the wound from an arrow which had been dipped in deadly curare poison. However, the survivors brought back a clue to El Dorado. They had been told by the Indians, 'where salt comes from, comes gold.' Quickly, the German bankers appointed a successor to Dalfinger, Georg Hohermuth. In 1535 Hohermuth set out with a party of 409 men to follow in Dalfinger's footsteps and find the source of salt and gold. After an appalling expedition lasting three years, he returned with a remnant of his party, to report failure.

Then, in 1536, a successful expedition, led by Gonzalez Jiminez de Queseda, started out from Venezuela. After a year of unimaginable hardship – the original force of 800 was down to 200 – the expedition reached the borders of lands where salt was abundant. Queseda conquered a number of villages, and made them reveal the source of their gold and emeralds.

A reluctant Indian led them to the village of Hunsa, 2440 metres above sea level. The villagers put up a fight, but they were no match for the determined gold-crazed Spaniards. The houses of Hunsa, made of wood or wickerwork, were lined with gold plates. The pillaging Spaniards discovered that most families hoarded gold and emeralds in cloth bags. Queseda, with 50 men was able to frighten several thousand Indians into parting with their entire fortune of more than 150 000 pesos of gold and 230 emeralds. There was even an El Dorado to fit the legend. The Chibcha Indians had a coronation ceremony where the new king was covered in gold dust, and pushed out into the centre of Lake Guatavita and then immersed, staying in the water until all the gold dust was washed away. Queseda, however, never believed that Hunsa was the real El Dorado and he mounted two more expeditions, but without success.

Even at the time of his first expedition a city of gold called Manoa was supposed to exist somewhere in South America, and this became the central point of the legend of El Dorado. This was the Manoa that Sir Walter Raleigh searched for. He had read that Orellana, one of Pizarro's lieutenants, had discovered an earthly paradise, filled with the most precious riches that man could desire. Another Spaniard, Martinez, confirmed this, insisting that he had lived in that very land for seven months, and he produced a map to prove it. On it he had drawn three mountains: one of gold, one of silver and a third of salt. In 1595, Raleigh led an expedition in search of the golden city, Manoa, and although he did not find it, he published an account of his adventures under the title, *The Discoverie of the large, rich and beautiful Empyre of Guiana, with a relation of the great and Golden Citie of Manoa*. To save his life while in prison, convicted of high treason, Raleigh offered to lead another expedition to El Dorado. The greedy king, James I, allowed him to finance his own expedition, and he set sail in 1617.

When he reached Trinidad Raleigh fell ill, but he sent his son and Laurence Keymis up the Orinoco in five small boats. In a brush with a Spanish garrison Sir Walter's son was killed, and Keymis, after returning with the tragic news, in turn killed himself because of Raleigh's reproaches. The expedition had no

Baron Humboldt, who searched for El Dorado.

choice but to return to England where Raleigh was arrested and then beheaded in October 1618.

Raleigh's failure to find El Dorado was no proof that it did not exist. His map showed Manoa as a city on Lake Parima. This was later disproved by Baron Humboldt, a German explorer and naturalist, who led several expeditions to find the legendary city of gold. Several times each century adventurers go in search of El Dorado. There is little doubt that an Englishman, Colonel Percy Fawcett, was searching for it when he disappeared in 1925, apparently murdered by Indians. His dream was probably as unrealistic as those of his predecessors: 'It is certain,' he wrote, 'that amazing ruins of ancient cities – ruins incomparably older than those of Egypt – exist in the far interior of the Matto Grosso.' Fawcett was never definite about what he had seen on his previous expeditions, but something was driving him on.

The Matto Grosso is still the largest area unexplored by modern man. It may be that the legendary City of Gold lies buried somewhere in Brazil's impenetrable jungles.

Sir Walter's son was killed in a brush with a Spanish garrison.

Colonel Percy Fawcett, who disappeared in the forest of the Matto Grosso.

Anna or Anastasia?

When the pain in her head became unbearable, she was lifted from the cart and carried in someone's arms.

It was 16 July, 1918. Anastasia was awakened in the middle of the night by a hammering on her bedroom door. A rough voice shouted in broken Russian, 'Get dressed, there's a disturbance in the town and shooting. It will be safer downstairs.' Quickly slipping into a skirt and white blouse, Anastasia hurried outside. A valuable pearl necklace given to her by her father was stitched into the hem of the skirt. It was a hot summer's night, so she did not bother to take her jacket, although it had diamonds concealed in its buttons.

Outside, her parents and sisters were being herded downstairs by the Red guards, her father carrying her brother in his arms. Alexei had always been a sickly child suffering from haemophilia, a rare blood disease. As they were directed into a cellar, Anastasia noticed that Demidova, her mother's lady in waiting, was with them, also the manservant, cook and their family doctor and friend, Dr Botkin. The whole household was there, except for young Leonid, the kitchen boy.

The single lamp threw grotesque shadows across the walls of the cellar. It was a heavily-vaulted room with a double window, protected by strong iron grating, set high in one wall. Outside, Anastasia could hear the roaring of a lorry engine being revved up. One of the most tragic acts in history was about to take place deep in the Ipatiev House in Ekaterinburg.

Anastasia as a young child. Overnight her carefree existence turned into one of horror.

At one end of the room Anastasia and her family were arranged according to strict protocol. Nicholas II, Tsar of All the Russias, sat in the centre, with his son, Alexei the Tsarevitch, seated on his right, and Dr Botkin standing next to them. Beside them sat the tsarina, Alexandra, Queen Victoria's grand-daughter. She was half fainting with fear. She had her four daughters – Olga, Tatiana, Maria and Anastasia, standing round her. Demidova, the manservant and the cook stood against the wall.

Yurovski, a brutal and ruthless officer in the Cheka, the Bolshevik secret police, stepped forward. His harsh voice cut across the silent tension of the room: 'Nicolai Alexandrovich, your followers tried to set you free. They failed however. Now you are going to be shot.'

'What!' cried the tsar, stunned and bewildered.

'This,' answered Yurovski, raising his revolver. The tsarina and one of her daughters crossed themselves. Yurovski opened fire at the tsar, killing him immediately. Yurovski's men, all Latvians and members of the Cheka, began to fire indiscriminately at the rest of the tsar's family. Victim after victim fell.

Ipatiev House, first and last home of the Romanovs.

The murdered Romanov family. From left to right: Olga, Maria, the tsar and tsarina, Anastasia, the tsarevitch Alexei and Tatiana.

In total silence the killers stared through the drifting gun smoke at their now still victims. There was a dreadful smell of blood and cordite. But Yurovski and his men, hardened criminals, began looting the bodies for rings, bracelets, gold watches and other valuables, as the reward for their butchery. With a haste suggesting a guilty conscience, they bundled their victims on to improvised stretchers and carried them out to the waiting lorry. In this haste Yurovski failed to check if they were all really dead.

Things were not going quickly enough, more guards were sent for to dispose of the bodies and clean up the cellar. Outside, in the pitch darkness, men were rushing about, hastily loading their grim burdens into the lorry, but in the confusion no one counted the number of bodies. This nightmare scene lasted for at least 20 minutes, then, at a sign from Yurovski, the lorry set off for its destination – a deserted mine deep in the woods. Here, the blood-stained corpses had petrol and sulphuric acid poured over them and were then cremated. Their ashes and remains were thrown down a pit. This was the end of the Romanov Dynasty, supreme rulers of Russia for 300 years. Or was it?

In 1917 the Bolshevik revolution had put first Kerensky, then Lenin in power, and the tsar and his family had found themselves prisoners. At the beginning they were held in one of the tsar's summer palaces, Tsarkoe Selo, but later they were whisked off to Tobolsk in Siberia. Finally they were taken to the Ipatiev House in Ekaterinburg. Plans had been made in Moscow for a public show trial of the tsar, but a counter revolutionary army was bearing down on Ekaterinburg, so these plans were changed rapidly. Orders came to shoot the whole of the Romanov family, together with all their retainers and then cover up all traces of the murder. Uncharacteristically, the murderers spared the kitchen boy, Leonid, on the night.

Later, a strange story began to circulate. There was a body missing. There is much evidence to support the belief that Anastasia did in fact escape, and many witnesses have come forward to testify to this. Certainly the Soviet government believed it. All their resources were thrown into a gigantic operation to search for the missing grand duchess, in an area ranging from the Baltic Sea to the borders of Romania and across Siberia. The search was very thorough and went to fantastic lengths. Houses were searched and a constant watch was kept on hospitals, especially the female wards. Still more men were thrown into the search. It was obvious that they were seeking a living person; a survivor of the Ekaterinburg massacre, around whom a counter revolution might form.

This photograph of Nicholas II and his children was taken shortly before their death.

They became desperate. Notices and posters were displayed on walls, army orders issued, people cross-examined, arrested and shot on the flimsiest of suspicions. Part of a notice addressed 'to the population and the army' read:

'During the execution of the sentence pronounced by the Ekaterinburg soviet on the Romanov family, certain persons in the firing squad acted insubordinately and made off with female members of the family, also taking valuables.'

Apparently they thought that there may have been more than one survivor.

There is a story that two members of the guard who had been called in to assist the murderers to load their victims aboard the lorry, bent over the blood-soaked figure of one of the young grand duchesses, Anastasia. She was still alive, and although it looked doubtful that she would survive the frightful wound in her head, the guards gently wrapped her in a blanket and carried her towards the lorry. It was unattended. So, after looking round to check that no one was behind them, they hurried into the darkness beyond the lorry's headlights to a small house about 180 metres up the lane from the Ipatiev House. Here, they put Anastasia to bed and hurried back before they were missed.

Unless they had been convinced that one of the tsar's daughters had escaped, the Bolsheviks would never have conducted such a long and extensive search.

Count Carl Bonde, one time head of the Swedish Red Cross mission to Siberia (set up during 1917–1918) wrote:

'In my capacity as Head of the Swedish Red Cross in Siberia, I was travelling in a special train during 1918. At some place, the name of which I have forgotten, the train was stopped and searched for the grand duchess Anastasia, the daughter of Tsar Nicholas II. The grand duchess was not on the train, however. No one knew where she had got to.'

Then in February 1920, a girl with papers in the name of Anna Tschaikovski, was pulled out of a canal in Berlin. She claimed to be Anastasia and said that she could remember being loaded into a farm cart, and having an agonizing pain in her head that came with every lurch of the unsprung vehicle. Her hair had been sticky with blood. All too clearly she could recall the scene in the cellar and hear the screams of her family. Her story was that as she drifted back to consciousness she became aware of the four people who were looking after her. The woman Maria, in her 40s, appeared to be the mother of the other three, Alexander, Sergei and Veronica. They told her that their name was Tschaikovski. The men had been in the Red Guard at Ekaterinburg.

The girl had vague recollections of travelling through dark pine forests and along lonely country roads for months on end – often in a high fever, and suffering from great pain in her head, in a raw wound in her arm, and in her face and mouth. When the pain in her head became unbearable, she was lifted from the cart and carried in someone's arms. More dead than alive, she hung on, often plagued by thirst as the water ran out. When winter came, her rescuers wrapped her in snow-covered sheets to reduce her fever. There were periods of bliss when they stayed on strange farms, free from the shaking of the unsprung cart. But there was always the fear of pursuit and discovery and the ever-present terror of betrayal.

Yet witnesses claim to have seen them and some helped them. One, a German prisoner of war trying to get back to Germany, claimed that he met a farm cart in the neighbourhood of Ekaterinburg, and travelled some way with it. There were two women sleeping in the straw, one of whom was wounded, and allegedly a grand duchess. Another German, Lieutenant-Colonel Hassenstein, the communications officer at a town on the River Bug, tells of an ox-drawn turnip cart crossing the pontoon bridge which was held by the Germans. When he learned that one of the tsar's daughters was on the cart he interceded with General Gillhausen, his superior officer, to allow it to cross.

An American, Sarsha Gregorian, helped the party cross the River Dniestr into Romania. Later he made a statement to the Bucharest police, translated and signed by Superintendent Héroua. It reads:

'Sarsha Gregorian states that . . . . . before crossing the Dniestr on his way from Russia to Romania (December 5 1918) he stayed at a monastery near the Romanian border. Also staying there was the Grand Duchess Anastasia, the youngest daughter of Tsar Nicholas II, who had been saved during the night of the murder by a Red Guard soldier, one of those guarding the Ipatiev House where the Imperial family were interned.'

Crossing the river at Rezina, the party met a tsarist Russian officer, who took them all in his car to Orhei. From there they were taken to Bucharest. Anna Tschaikovski said that at last she felt a sense of elation. She was free. Here, on Romanian soil, she was safe from the Bolsheviks who had murdered her family.

The hidden pearl necklace was quickly sold to raise money for herself and the Tschaikovskis to live on. Then something happened which she was later to claim turned many of her mother's relatives against her. She had a child and Alexander Tschaikovski was the father. The couple married but the damage had been done. It made it impossible for many of the German and Middle European princelings to accept her as a relative. A woman who had got herself in such a position would never be allowed to take her place in the dwindling royal courts of Europe.

Soon after the marriage, fate struck Anna yet another blow. Alexander was shot in the street by Bolshevik agents, according to the distraught widow. With nothing to keep her in Bucharest, she set out for Berlin accompanied by Sergei. The child had been placed in an orphanage under an assumed name and was never subsequently traced. In Berlin Sergei disappeared, and Anna, on the point of a complete psychological breakdown, threw herself into a canal in an attempt at suicide.

When Anna Tschaikovski was pulled out of the canal, people began to question her but she refused to answer. People would never believe that she was the Grand Duchess Anastasia, and should they ever discover that she was Russian they would hand her over to the Bolsheviks. So, she refused to give her name. The questioning became more insistent, but still she refused to speak. After a few weeks at the Elizabeth Hospital, she was sent to Dalldorf Mental Hospital as she was obviously mad! The Berlin police commenced their enquiries. By now it was 30 March 1920.

A time of appalling suffering began for Anna. Placed in a public ward, she was surrounded by the mentally sick, all anxious to air their own particular obsession. Most of the time she spent in bed, her face turned to the wall. Klara Maria Peuthert, who had worked as a governess for the ladies at Tsarkoe Selo was also in the hospital. She immediately thought that she recognized Anna as one of the tsar's daughters, but mistook her for Tatiana. Klara Peuthert was released after a short time, and immediately the Russian émigré circles began buzzing with the news that one of the tsar's daughters was still alive. They began to visit Anna, singly and in groups. Once the patient was shown a photograph of an old lady, and burst out, 'That's my grandmother.'

Baroness Isa Buxhoevden, once the tsarina's lady in waiting, was sent by Princess Irene of Prussia, Anastasia's aunt, to visit Mrs Tschaikovski, but she failed to recognize her. The grand duchess, due to her suffering, would have looked very much older than her 21 years. All her front teeth had apparently been knocked out by a rifle blow causing her cheeks to fall in. Isa Buxhoevden was quite adamant however, and her evidence did much to discredit Anna's claims.

Released from Dalldorf after two years, Anna went to live with Baron and Baroness Kleist, Russian émigrés. A German police officer, Inspector Grünberg, who had been assigned to the investigation of the woman claiming to be a grand duchess, began to take a personal interest in the girl and managed to persuade her to stay with him and his family on their country estate. Meanwhile, the émigrés had split into two camps: those who believed the woman was Anastasia and those who believed her to be an imposter. The royal relatives, who might so easily have solved the question between them, sat on the fence.

Princess Irene who eventually rejected Anna.

An extract from one of Inspector Grünberg's reports reads:

'. . Feeling that there was a historical mystery here comparable to that of the Man in the Iron Mask, I decided, in agreement with Baron Kleist, to take the young lady for three weeks to my estate at Fünken-muhle near Neuhoff-Teltow. Staying two years at Dalldorf had completely shattered her nerves. Moreover, she had been wounded in the head (skull battered by blows from a rifle) which led to a certain mental derangement, and in addition there was a mental instability in the family on her mother's side. She claims with great assurance to be the late tsar's youngest daughter, Anastasia, and has given descriptions of the Imperial family's stay at Tobolk and Ekaterinberg, as well as of family life at court, which presuppose exact knowledge . . . She also made precise statements about the night of the murder and the general massacre.'

Quite apart from her mental condition, Anna was now becoming seriously ill, a swelling on her chest was growing bigger and bigger and she was running a temperature. It was another cruel twist of fate that Anastasia's aunt, Princess Irene, should have chosen just that time to visit her, incognito. Although later claiming to recognize her aunt immediately she spoke, Anna refused both to talk to her and the offer to accompany her aunt to her estate at Hemmel-mark.

Princess Irene, for her part, came out with a positive statement:

'The hair, forehead and eyes are Anastasia's but the mouth and chin are not. I cannot say that it isn't her.'

With her mouth and face smashed in by the butt of a rifle, the lower part of Anastasia's face might well have looked different. Anastasia or not, the woman had thrown away her best chance of being accepted. From that day onwards, Princess Irene refused to have anything to do with the whole affair.

It was then discovered that Anna had tuberculosis of the breastbone, which also attacked the left elbow. (Consumption was a common complaint on the tsar's side of the family.) Operation followed operation with little success, until, given only a fortnight to live, she underwent more drastic surgery from which she recovered. But from then on she was never completely well – physically or mentally.

One by one the tsarina's relatives came to study the girl who claimed to be Anastasia, but they were always met with rudeness and went away either puzzled, or convinced that the woman was an imposter. One stumbling block to acceptance was the fact that she could not speak English, the language most commonly used among the tsar's family. She could not read or write, and claimed not to speak Russian. However, she fell into simple traps laid for her by the émigrés. Often they would talk disparagingly about her among themselves in Russian. Her caustic comments, spoken in German, left no doubt that she had understood every word.

A list of identifying marks on Anna was sent to Anastasia's uncle Ernest, the Grand Duke of Hesse.

1 Bunions on both feet, specially marked on the right foot. (Anastasia had bunions on her feet in the same place.)
2 A small white scar on the shoulder blade from a cauterized mole. (A similar scar was shown in Anastasia's medical records.)
3 The scar of a laceration or bruise at the root of the middle finger on the left hand. (This was claimed to have been caused by a footman slamming the carriage door too soon. Although this story was denied by Anna's opponents, a former lady-in-waiting verified it.)
4 A small indistinct scar on the right of the forehead. (Anastasia used to have her hair cut short and combed over the forehead to hide a scar caused by a fall.)
5 A scar behind the right ear established by doctors to be a graze from a bullet.
A radiograph of Anna's head was also sent, which showed serious skull injuries.

A curt reply stated that it was out of the question that any of the tsar's daughters should be alive. Unfortunately Anna had mentioned having seen the Grand Duke of Hesse in Russia in 1916, when the two countries were still at war with each other. Rumour had it that he had gone there to negotiate a separate peace with his brother-in-law, the tsar, on behalf of Hesse, Saxony and Bavaria. It was a rumour that the grand duke had been trying to live down ever since. Could this be a reason for the flat rejection of his supposed niece?

And so the controversy raged on. Some people accepted Mrs Tschaikovski as the Grand Duchess Anastasia; others flatly rejected her, including most of the immediate relatives and people who had been intimate with the tsar's family, among them the tutor. As time went on

One by one, the tsarina's relatives came to study the girl who claimed to be Anastasia.

Anastasia's uncle, Ernest, Grand Duke of Hesse. Was he really trying to negotiate a separate peace? Was this why he flatly rejected Anna?

105

Is there any similarity between Anna Anderson (above) and this family snapshot of the Grand Duchess Anastasia (below)?

Anna was able to 'remember' more and more intimate details of her childhood in Russia, but then an added complication arose. Anna had made the following statement:

'I, the Grand Duchess Anastasia Niko-laievna, youngest daughter and only surviving child of the late Nicholas II and Empress Alexandra of Russia, declare herewith that after our family had left St Petersburg and been banished to Ekaterinburg in Siberia, and shortly before my father and the rest of my family were killed, he informed my three sisters and myself that before the outbreak of the World War he had deposited 5 000 000 roubles each for the four of us with the Bank of England.'

But the Bank of England denied ever having held any funds deposited by the tsar, in any name. Anna altered her original statement to read: 'with an English bank' – an understandable mistake – but still the money has not been traced.

Anna spent some time in America during the late 1920s, and it was there that she changed her name to Anna Anderson. It was during her stay there, that members of Anastasia's family, 12 to be precise out of 44, issued a joint statement, which they all signed, to the Associated Press, rejecting her. Significantly, they were the 12 who, if all the tsar's daughters were dead including Anastasia, might have had claims to a possible fortune in England.

The world's newspapers took sides and have been doing so ever since. Countless books have been written on the subject, for and against Anna Anderson. Legal actions have been taken on both sides and a film has been made about the mysterious claimant, starring Ingrid Bergman and Yul Brynner.

After the Second World War, Anna Anderson moved into an old army hut in the Black Forest, in Germany, where she lived quietly with a single companion. Then in 1974 she married an American and went back to live in the United States of America.

Could the Grand Duchess Anastasia really have escaped that dreadful holocaust, way back in 1918? Will her authenticity ever be proved?

The legend of Anastasia's escape captured the imagination of Hollywood, where it was turned into a film starring Ingrid Bergman and Yul Brynner.

Flight 19

The tension in the tower mounted as the radioman took down the message, still badly distorted by static.

The sun was shining on a bright winter's day as Lieutenant Charles Taylor lifted his Navy Grumman TBM-3 Avenger torpedo bomber off the runway at the Naval Air Station at Fort Lauderdale, Florida. It was about 2.00 pm on 5 December, 1945. There were only scattered clouds , the temperature was 18°C and pilots who had flown earlier that day reported ideal flying weather. Circling base, Lieutenant Taylor closely watched each of the four pot-bellied Avengers of his flight lumber along the tarmac and somehow take to the air. Not the prettiest of aircraft he thought to himself.

Nevertheless, by 2.10 pm his flight, Flight 19, were all airborne and ranged each side of their leader. Glancing left and right he checked that each aircraft was on station – not that he would have expected anything otherwise. The four officer pilots had all been flying for some time as had the seven enlisted crew members. There were usually two to each plane, but today they were one crew member short as one man had requested removal from flying status because of a premonition, and his request had been granted. (A later study of the pre-flight personnel check showed that Flight 19 took off with a full complement. Was this a mistake, or had a mysterious passenger boarded at the last moment?) Taylor himself, with Pacific combat experience behind him, had over 2500 hours flying time to his credit. He checked plane to plane intercom and gyro and magnetic compass bearings. They were all in order. There was no reason why they should not be.

The flight was a straightforward training exercise, and flying time for the mission had been calculated at two hours. Each aircraft carried enough fuel to enable it to cruise over 1500 kilometres. On this excercise, Flight 19 was to fly 260 kilometres due east, 65 kilometres to the north, and then back to base following a southwest course. Lieutenant Taylor had done it several times already. He led his planes to Chicken Shoals, north of Bimini, where they were to make practice runs on a target hulk.

'Target ahead.' Down he went, skimming the smooth surface of the sea as he lined his Avenger up for a torpedo run. Glancing over his shoulder he made sure that his flight was following him, line astern. The runs completed, he ordered the flight to break off and the aircraft began to head east – out into the Atlantic.

The duty radioman at Fort Lauderdale Naval Air Station tower had for some time been expecting contact from the planes regarding estimated time of arrival and landing instructions. He had heard nothing. Then, at about 3.45 pm, a message came through from Flight 19, distorted by an unusual amount of static: 'Flight Leader calling tower. Flight Leader calling tower. This is an emergency . . . We seem to be off course. We cannot see land . . . repeat . . . we cannot see land.'

Tower 'What is your position?'

Flight Leader 'We are not sure of our position. We cannot be sure just where we are. We seem to be lost.'

Tower 'Assume bearing due west.' (This would have taken the aircraft back to the Florida Coast.)

Flight Leader 'We don't know which way is west. Everything is wrong . . . strange . . . we can't be sure of any direction. Even the ocean doesn't look as it should.'

The radio went silent.

At about 3.40 pm, the senior flight instructor at Ford Lauderdale, airborne at the time, picked up a plane to plane intercom message from Flight 19.

'Powers. Report your compass readings. I don't know where we are. We must have got lost after that last turn.'

Mystified, the senior flight instructor made contact with Lieutenant Taylor. Faintly he heard the flight leader reply: 'Both my compasses are out. I am trying to find Fort Lauderdale, Florida. I am sure I'm in the Keys, but I don't know how far down.'

'Fly north with the sun on your portside, that will bring you back to Fort Lauderdale,' the instructor told him.

Later, at about 4.25 pm, the tower picked up

another message: 'We have just passed over a small island. No other land in sight.' The flight was certainly not over the Keys which are a string of small islands just south of Florida. It was lost!

Radio contact became increasingly bad as the static built up, but disjointed and highly disturbing phrases were picked up over the plane to plane intercom: 'Fuel shortage'; Fuel for only 75 miles [120 kilometres]'; '75 miles-an-hour winds'; 'Every compass, gyro and magnetic showing a different reading. Going crazy.'

Base command had by now become very concerned as the news spread that Flight 19 had encountered an emergency. Rescue craft were despatched from Banana River Naval Station, including a monster Martin Mariner flying boat with a crew of 13. Minutes after take off the tower received a message from Lieutenant Cone, one of the Mariner's crew. Arriving in the general area where Flight 19 was presumed to be, the flying boat had run into strong winds above 1800 metres. This was the last message received from the rescue plane. It had disappeared!

The tower again made contact with the Avengers, but Lieutenant Taylor was no longer the leader of the flight. He had turned over command to Captain Stiver, a senior Marine pilot. The tension in the tower mounted as the radioman took down the message, still badly distorted by static.

'We are not sure where we are . . . . We think we must be 225 miles [about 360 kilometres] north east of base. . . We must be in the Gulf of Mexico.' Stiver decided to make a turn of 180° and head back to Florida. Horrified, the senior personnel of Fort Lauderdale stared at the giant radio transmitter. The transmission became fainter and fainter. This could mean only one thing – the flight had made a wrong turn and was heading due east, straight out into the vast wastes of the Atlantic. No further message was received from Flight 19 training mission, although the Naval Air Station at Miami picked up the faint echo of a message: 'FT . . . FT . . .' which was part of the flight's call sign, Taylor's plane being FT-28. This began yet another mystery. Miami intercepted this message at 7.00 pm – 2 hours after the planes should have run out of fuel!

Airborne Grumman Avengers.

Something like panic gripped Lauderdale and a gigantic search by sea and air was put into operation. Wild ideas flew round the control centre: 'Enemy attack', although World War II had been over for several months; attack by a new enemy; even the never-mentioned expression, UFO was whispered. Why had the compasses gone haywire?

Called off at nightfall, one of the most intensive ever search efforts began again at dawn. There were 240 planes supplemented by 67 planes from the aircraft carrier Solomons, 4 destroyers, a number of submarines, 18 coast guard vessels, hundreds of private planes, yachts and boats, all scouring an area of 984 000 square kilometres. They found nothing.

Not a scrap of wreckage, not a single life raft was found. There were no oil slicks – nothing. Despite a constant watch, no flotsam was washed up on the beaches of Florida and the Bahamas. The mystery deepened. Had the aircraft made forced landings? Surely there would have been some survivors. Grumman Avengers would stay afloat for 90 seconds, and the crews were trained to abandon aircraft in 60 seconds. Life rafts were obtained from outside the planes, so in the event of a forced landing they would almost certainly float. Yet none were found. The Naval Department was faced with an undeniable fact. Six aircraft had completely disappeared without a trace.

A Board of Enquiry was set up to examine the reasons for the disappearances. It came to no definite conclusions although it did consider court-martialling the instrument officer. However, he was later exonerated when it was established that all the instruments had been checked out before take off. An information officer attached to the Board, said after the Enquiry, ' . . Members of the Board of Enquiry were not able to make even a good guess as to what had happened.' In all innocence another Board Member stated, 'They vanished as completely as if they had flown to Mars.' Unwittingly he had introduced the element of space travel into

the disappearance of Flight 19. The press latched on to this and the number of UFO sightings greatly increased. Not only did the press start to delve, but serious observers and investigators began to show an interest in this area. The phrase, 'Bermuda Triangle' was coined. This denotes a section of the Western Atlantic, roughly triangular in shape, off the south east coast of the United States. It extends from Bermuda in the north to southern Florida, and then east through the Bahamas past Puerto Rico to roughly the 40° west meridian and back to Bermuda. Close investigation turned up some very disquieting facts and not a few theories, some wild, others all too credible.

Aircraft crews were trained to transfer quickly to life rafts from which they could be rescued.

Explanations are varied and some are far-fetched.

The 19000-ton USS Cyclops *which vanished without a trace.*

Edgar Cayce, who believed that some crystal power sources remained from Atlantis.

The facts and figures speak for themselves. Over 100 planes and ships have literally vanished into thin air, many of them outside the original 'Bermuda Triangle', and most of them since the ill-fated Flight 19 in 1945. More than 1000 lives have been lost over the same period – the people have vanished, that is. These disappearances are still continuing, despite every precaution being taken. Some aircraft have even vanished while receiving landing instructions from their destination airport. No explanation, no reason, no 'May Day'. It is as if they had flown into a hole in the sky.

The history of vanishing ships goes back further, and ancient mariners have related tales of ghost ships floating crewless in the Sargasso Sea, 'The Sea of Fear', (part of the Atlantic Ocean in the 'Bermuda Triangle'), deserted and still, in the middle of the terrible beds of seaweed. Ships such as the *Marine Sulphur Queen*, a 120 metres-long freighter, and the *USS Cyclops*, 19 000 tons, with 309 people aboard, have simply vanished without a trace. Others have been found drifting within the 'Triangle', without a living soul aboard other than the occasional ship's pet. Although it may be significant that in one instance a talking parrot disappeared along with the crew!

Explanations are varied and some are far-fetched. Sudden tidal waves caused by earthquakes; attacks by sea monsters; fireballs which blow up aircraft; a time-space warp leading to another dimension are some of them. One fanciful theory blames the disappearances on flying and submarine UFOs, manned by intelligences from space or the 'future', who capture and kidnap people to obtain specimens of current earth inhabitants and examples of our technology. A psychic who died in 1944, Edgar Cayce the 'sleeping prophet', believed that the fabled lost continent of Atlantis sank beneath the sea off Bimini (the position of many of the unaccountable disappearances), and that the crystal power sources used by the Atlanteans were still exerting an influence over modern compasses and electrical equipment.

People continue to give natural explanations for the disappearances, but the fact remains that a large number of planes and ships have vanished from the face of the Earth – without trace!

Have we lived before?

She solemnly informed him that in previous lives he had been a Moor and later a French alchemist.

Is this our first life, or have we lived before as different people? The late Arnold Bloxham, a hypnotherapist, was convinced that people have more than one life. He made more than 100 tape-recordings of ordinary people giving amazingly detailed accounts of their previous lives. He first became aware of the possibility of reincarnation when he was a small child. In dreams and nightmares he visited past ages, people and places totally unknown to him. These dreams were so vivid that he used to wake up screaming in terror, and someone had to hold his hand when he went to sleep, because he was afraid of what was going to happen next.

Much later in life, while walking in the Cotswolds, he suddenly came upon a road that had appeared in many of his dreams. He knew with certainty that:

'if we went down the steep hill, turned to the right, in about half a mile or so [about 1 kilometre] we'd come to two towers and iron gates.

'And we did this and came to Sudely Castle and I realized that was where I had once lived – behind those iron gates.'

At a later visit to the castle he was able to show his wife round the castle without a guide, leading her to places which he 'knew' were there, yet he had never been inside Sudely Castle in his life before – that is, his present life!

Arnall Bloxham grew up in Pershore in Worcestershire, where even as a boy at Worcester Royal Grammar School, he was interested in hypnotism, in those days at the turn of the century, known as 'mesmerism'. His first success as a hypnotherapist occurred when he cured a fellow pupil's headache. He had hoped to become a doctor but this was forestalled by the outbreak of the First World War, and at 18 he joined the Royal Navy, serving aboard minesweepers. His hopes were finally shattered when he went down with typhoid fever. As a potential carrier of the disease he could never work in a hospital, so he turned to hypnotherapy. He had considerable success over the years, and in 1972 he became President of the British Society of Hypnotherapists. Today hypnotherapy is recognized, but this has not always been the case and Arnall Bloxham has encountered his share of prejudice and suspicion.

At three week intervals he would hold 'sess-

Sudely Castle in the Cotswolds. Arnall Bloxham was able to show his wife around the castle without the help of a guide, although he had never been there before.

ions' at his home in Cardiff for friends and a sprinkling of strangers, when he would play tape-recordings of people he had hypnotized and taken back to 'previous existences'. Although he always encouraged question and discussion, he never gave demonstrations, saying: 'I strongly disapprove of stage hypnotism and that sort of thing. It's too serious a subject and too dangerous to be used in this way.'

Throughout his life, Bloxham believed in reincarnation, but it was not until late in his career that he began to experiment with regression to a past life. It was not in idle curiosity, but arose from the treatment of a patient. This patient, a chemist, was a chronic hypochondriac, and handling so many pills and medicines did nothing to improve his morbid concern with imaginary illnesses. Bloxham listed the chemist's imaginary complaints:

'When he came to see me he was in a terrible state. I wrote down a list of all the things he said he had wrong with him and I thought, "This fellow seems to have everything the matter with him that I have ever heard of."

'Anyway, I put him under hypnosis and eventually cured him of all this hypochondria. But then his wife said, "There's one thing remaining. He's terribly afraid that he is going to die. . . . He's afraid to go to sleep in case he won't wake up."'

Knowing he would be unable to convince the chemist, under hypnosis, that he was not going to die, Bloxham hit on another solution.

'I told his wife: "Yes, I can cure him. I'll put him under hypnosis and make him realize that he has lived before. Therefore, if he lived before, he'll live again."'

Under hypnosis the chemist told Bloxham he was the son of a 17th century sea-captain who, together with his wife, died in the Great Plague of London.

Encouraged by this, Bloxham began to experiment with questioning techniques, and by remaining neutral he found he could help the hypnotized subjects to relive their former existences in great detail. Over the years he built up an impressive library of tape-recordings covering many eras and many dif-

ferent life styles. He came to recognize true happenings from fantasy built round some forgotten historical story heard long ago.

'I have asked hypnotized people questions about a period of history which they know very well. But the answers I have had differ completely from what they've read about it in this life. If I suggest anything to them, which may be historically acceptable, but which is contrary to what is happening in their previous life, they will deny it.'

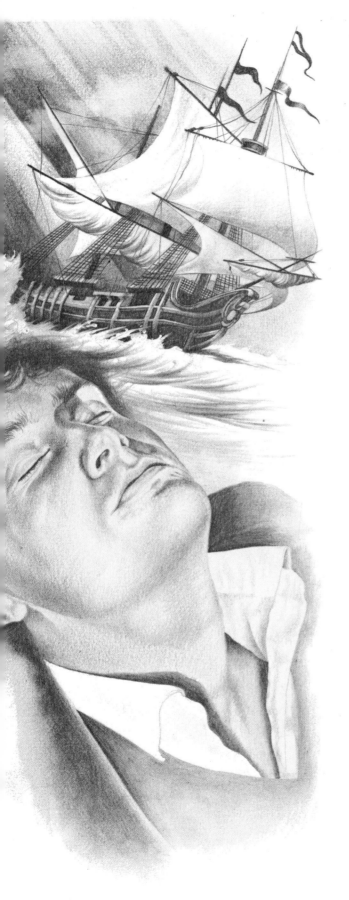

Arnall Bloxham, who really wanted to be a doctor. As a potential carrier of typhoid fever, he could never work in a hospital.

In 1974 the work of Bloxham caught the attention of the BBC. One of their producers, Jeffrey Iverson, was sent to interview him to see if it would be worthwhile making a television programme based on the results of the hypnotherapist's experiments. He wrote an account of his investigations in his book, *More Lives than One.*

Arnall Bloxham turned out to be a small man in his late 70s, carefully dressed with a rose in his buttonhole. He was quiet, precise and obviously inspired confidence. He had small, impassive features. But Iverson's first reaction was far from favourable. A middle-aged woman, who turned out to be a psychic medium, served tea in a lounge in which stood a handsome four-poster bed, and on a wall the deathmask of the nobleman who was supposed to have slept in it. At a word from Bloxham, she put her hand on Iverson's forehead, closed her eyes, and solemnly informed him that in previous lives he had been a Moor and later a French alchemist. Both lives had ended violently. Then Bloxham began to play parts of some of his tapes: a woman who had lived as a Jewess in York, a victim of the 12th century massacre of Jews; a man who had witnessed the Great Fire of London in 1666.

The name of someone he knew in Cardiff cropped up. John Pike, a television cameraman, had been for a number of years a local press photographer. He, with a reporter, had interviewed Bloxham for a newspaper article many years ago. This man, to Iverson's certain knowledge, was the last person to be drawn into a fanciful charade.

Over a drink with Pike, Iverson began rapidly to change his attitude. Yes, Pike did remember visiting Bloxham in 1957. Yes, he had allowed himself to be hypnotized and the resulting tape had puzzled him ever since. Somewhat chastened, Jeffrey Iverson made up his mind to see Bloxham again, make a full investigation of the Bloxham tapes and allow the outcome to speak for itself.

Catherine of Aragon, first wife of Henry VIII. Jane Evans remembered vividly her life as a Spanish handmaid to Queen Catherine during a previous existence.

Arnall Bloxham was willing, so Iverson decided to promote a serious and prolonged investigation of a woman who had regressed six times and could talk fluently about her six previous lives. The woman wished her real name to be withheld so she took the name Jane Evans.

Her previous lives had been spent as the wife of Titus, a tutor at Roman York then called Eboracum; a Jewess at the time of the York Massacre in 1190; a maidservant at Bourges, in France, in the 15th century; a Spanish handmaiden to Catherine of Aragon; a poor sewing girl in the age of Queen Anne in London and a nun in a convent in Maryland, USA, at the turn of the century. Jane had started her regressions because she had told Bloxham that she had always been interested in reading about Greece and Tibet, but had no idea why. Sensing an affinity with these countries, Bloxham had persuaded her to be hypnotized. But although she regressed to six former lives, she never mentioned Tibet or Greece.

The first tape to be made by Jane Evans was her life as a Jewess in medieval York. The date is 1189. Her name is Rebecca. She is the wife of a wealthy Jewish moneylender, 'Joseph of the seed of Ezekiel'. She and her husband are both aged 40 and have two children, Joseph, 18, and Rachel, aged 11. They live in a large stone house at the north of the City, it has eight rooms.

There is no evidence that a Jewish community lived in that part of York at the time, but today there is a municipal car park covering an area called Jewbury, and records of a Jewish cemetery there date from 1230. So it is likely that a generation before this, Jews could have lived in the area.

Although her husband wears costly clothes, they must not appear to be costly, the Jews in York are hated and despised for their wealth and are forced to wear yellow badges over their hearts.

Bloxham asked her: 'Do you mind having to wear these badges?'

Rebecca replies, 'Yes. They mock us because of our religion. They mock us because we cleanse ourselves, because we teach our sons, because we won't eat unclean food. They make us wear these patches on our clothes to show we are Jews.'

Professor Barrie Dobson of York University, an authority on Jewish history of this period, (a highly specialized subject not very well covered in popular literature) points out it is a known fact that from the year 1215 every Jew in Christendom, on papal authority, had to wear a badge so that they might be recognized as such. He goes on to say, 'It is quite conceivable that in parts of England some sort of badge of the sort she mentions might have been imposed on York Jews in the late 12th century.'

But now on the tape, Jane's knowledge becomes more detailed, and unlikely to have been read previously. Asked if she herself is happy, Rebecca replies that they are happy as a family, but are worried that the uprisings in London, Chester and Lincoln against the Jews might spread to York. Between Pentecost and Passover, a plague visited the City in which 200 Christians died, but no Jews. Naturally the people of York blamed the Jews.

It is a historical fact that there were uprisings in London and Lincoln, a large Jewish centre,

but there is not one recorded in Chester. However, there was one in Colchester, so was Rebecca just confusing the names, or was there also, an as yet unrecorded incident at Chester?

'Where would they be if it were not for us Jews?' asks Rebecca. 'They borrow our money to build their cathedrals and finance their wars in Ireland.'

It is almost certain that Henry II financed a war in Ireland, under the leadership of his son, John, with money he borrowed from the Jews.

The tape continues.

Bloxham: Who is the king who borrowed this money?

Rebecca: Henry Plantagenet (*pause*); he is a good king. He is good to the Jews. He helps us when we have to take our cases to the courts for the money that is owed us. In return we give him ten (*pause*) ten parts of the money that we gather back.'

Henry, according to historians did offer his protection to the Jews, for payment.

Rebecca's next replies show far more detailed and little-known knowledge of the Jewish history of the period.

Bloxham: Have you a synagogue?

Rebecca: Yes.

Bloxham: Perhaps it's a small one?'

Rebecca: Yes, they do not allow us very much. We are not recognized by them at all. . . . A Jew is not allowed to enter the army or hold land under feudal tenure, so what else can we do but lend money. We are not allowed to enter the army or go into trade, what else can we do?

Bloxham: Have there been any happenings lately?

Rebecca: Yes. A priest from the Christian Pope came, asking — came to the market place — asking men to sew crosses on to their robes and go to fight the infidels who have taken Jerusalem. And he told them to raise up their arms against the infidels and to join the armies — to join the armies in the Holy Land.

Bloxham: Did you see this representative of the Pope?

Rebecca: Yes.

Bloxham: What was he like?

Rebecca: Just a priest.

Bloxham: Do you know his name?

Rebecca: Massotti (*pause*) Massotti — And when he said 'take up your arms against the infidels,'

Jews trapped in the castle killed themselves rather than fall into the hands of the York mob.

123

the people of the crowd said, 'What about the infidels in York? All Jews are infidels.' And we are frightened, we are frightened (*pause*). My husband has sent money out of York to our uncle in Lincoln in case something terrible happens. King Henry is good to us, but King Henry is getting old – where would we be if it were anyone but Henry?

This almost certainly refers to the events leading up to the Third Crusade, which began within the year, under the next King of England, Richard Coeur de Lion. Historically it is known that a mass hysteria had been whipped up against the infidels, mainly by the Church – Jews being included among the infidels, and there were numerous riots and killings. But no evidence was found for a priest called Massotti.

Professor Dobson suggests that the York moneylending community may have been an offshoot of the Lincoln one. Strangely enough there is evidence of a leader of the York Jewish community called Joseph or 'Josce' of York, a wealthy moneylender. Could this Joseph have been the husband of Rebecca? But Joseph was a common Jewish name of the period.

Rebecca goes on to describe the family packing their valuables, ready to flee to London at a moment's notice. They have, along with most of the Jews, fortified their house, but have little hope of holding out for any length of time. Benjamin, their neighbour, tells them his father has been murdered in London. Rebecca is reluctant to leave York but says, '. . . so many awful things have happened. My husband will not tell me a lot of them, but I hear whispers about what has happened to some Jews. An old Jew called Isaac in Coney Street, he was murdered – he was murdered. Before they murdered him they made him eat pork and they poured holy water on his head and then they murdered him. And we are frightened of what they will do to us and our children. We will have to leave.'

HENRY II. 1154–1189.

King Henry II, who borrowed money from the Jews to finance his war in Ireland. He was more sympathetic towards them than most people of the time.

Rebecca goes on to talk about a young man called Mabelise who borrowed money and refused to pay it back. 'Mabelise. He hates us even more . . . We have fortified – we have fortified our windows and our doors and our courtyard doors. And we are always on watch. (*Pause*) Some of us have even taken off our yellow patches and go about the city at night to collect our debts, because we are frightened.'

Chronicles of the period relate how one Richard Malebisse (almost identical with Rebecca's Mabelise) was 'the arch-conspirator against the Jews', and led the massacre. He was called, 'Richard rightly called Mala Bestia or evil beast' by the medieval chronicler William of Newburgh.

It is known that a Jew was murdered in Coney Street at that time. It is also known that Benedict, a wealthy Jew from York and a close friend of Joseph of York was killed during a riot in London. Now Benedict was known to have had sons, might Benjamin have been one of these? Chronicles mention the sacking of Benedict's house in York, by an armed mob who broke in, killed all the inhabitants, including Benedict's widow and children, and made off with the treasure found there.

Rebecca's account tallies exactly with this and has a startling ring of truth about it. 'Yes. Yes, we all had to go. They came to the house of Benjamin next to us and we could hear the screams and smell the smoke. And we had to go. My husband and our son carrying money on their back in sacks – we had to go – we fled. (*Pause*) We wanted to go to the castle – we went through the back way to get to the castle but they were pursuing us so my husband slit a sack of silver and let it pour into the road so the people pursuing us would stop pursuing us and pick up the silver so that we could get a bit ahead of them. . .

'And when we got to the castle they wouldn't let us in – and they wouldn't let us in except just inside the wall . . . all the people crowded outside shouting to us to come out . . . telling us to come out and be killed. We were infidels, and asking if we had crucified any little boys and awful things – terrible things they were shouting at us. . . .

'We got out of the castle and we took shelter in a Christian church . . . there was a priest and a clerk in this church and we held them and bound them and told them we wouldn't hurt them as long as they didn't tell people we were there – and we were down in the cellars – down below the church . . . We have lost all our money. . . . We have had to give most of it away to get out of the castle. . . .

'But we are in their church and God's house is still God's house – but if they find us here they will surely kill us. But we must shelter – my husband is tired, his leg is wounded and injured – we must rest – we are hungry. . . .

'We can still hear them coming – we can see the flames. . . . We can hear them – still hear them screaming and we're frightened . . . my husband has gone to see if he can find food for us . . . and my son has gone with him . . . we can hear horses. Horses coming nearer and nearer and nearer – nearer. . . . we can hear the screaming and the shouting and the crying – ''burn the Jews, burn the Jews, burn the Jews.'' '

It was unlikely that Rebecca could have been murdered in the crypt of a church. The massacre, when about 150 Jews had been killed, had taken place in the castle, where many of the Jews, desperate, had cut the throats of their wives and children and then committed suicide themselves. The remainder at the end of the seige had been offered their lives in return for accepting the Christian faith. But when they came out they too were murdered.

The investigators began to search for the church in which Rebecca had sheltered. This is where Rebecca's story has a serious weakness. Of the 40 odd churches that had been in York at the time of the massacre, about half still remained, but not one of them had a crypt! Eventually it was established from Rebecca's description, that only one – St Mary's, Castlegate – could possibly be the church in which Rebecca hid, but it certainly had no crypt. Then, by an incredible coincidence, it was decided to turn St Mary's into a museum. During the renovations workmen uncovered a crypt with Roman and Anglo-Saxon pillars and masonry.

Had the whole story been a fantasy, or could Rebecca have been right? It has been argued that if it had in fact been fantasy, then Rebecca would have stuck to the generally accepted events that happened in the castle. But, by choosing a previously unknown situation, only confirmed by chance rebuilding, she strengthened the validity of her story.

But the intriguing question remains. How could an ordinary housewife in her late 30s, not over-given to reading history, know the history of the Jews of York in so much detail and express it so vividly? It does not stop there. Jane Evans produced five other tape-recordings, each one as equally detailed and accurate as the York one. How could she possibly know so much about everyday life in so many widely differing periods?

Jane Evans is only one of many, many others who have recorded on tape their detailed experiences in another life. The mind is still largely unexplored territory, and very few psychologists would be foolhardy enough to sweep away, as nonsense, any unusual excursions into the unknown. However, it is normal in everyday psychology for patients to regress, to live again, some scene from a part of their present life, so why not past life? We are still left with our first question. Is this our first life? There is some evidence to suggest that the answer could be no.

The grim castle keep, perched on its high knoll in the centre of York, still carries memories of the Jewish massacre when about 150 people died.

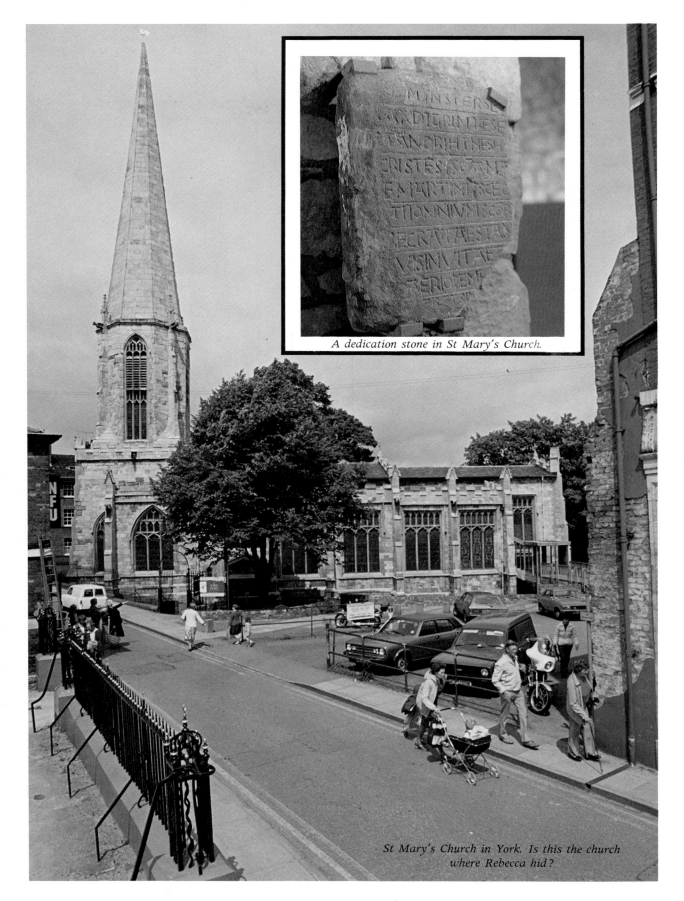

A dedication stone in St Mary's Church.

St Mary's Church in York. Is this the church where Rebecca hid?

The Loch Ness Monster

If the monster was not a lesser rorqual, what was it?

Is there a monster lurking in the murky depths of Loch Ness? Superstitious Scotsmen, since earliest times, have needed no convincing that *each uisage*, the fabled 'water horse', haunts the dark brackish water of the loch. Tales of the weird beastie were handed down from generation to generation until gradually a legend was built up that still intrigues people today.

On winter nights, with the wind howling down the Great Glen, people would frighten each other with stories of monsters which, as the whisky jar went round, became increasingly lurid. For hundreds of years these tales were not taken seriously, particularly as many Highlanders referred to the monster as a water kelpie (water spirit). This curious mixture of fact and supernatural fantasy was put down to the gift of the Highlander to tell a good story. An overheated imagination can make a great deal from moonlight rippling across windswept water, and floating logs silhouetted against the sunset.

However, too many eerie stories have come down over the years for all of them to be dismissed as superstitious nonsense, though some of them are a little hard to believe! Once, many hundreds of years ago, a family settled on a small island in the loch, and built 'ane strength house to keep the principall men and their kin and friends from enemies.' The chronicle of 1590 goes on to say:

' . . . . it fortuned on a tyme that ane monstrous beast being in that litle Logh, the most pairt of these Inhabitants being in this Illand, it was overwhelmit and destroyed by that terrible and most fearful Monstrous beast, and so they all were perished and devoured.'

The recorder of this story, Timothy Pont, insisted that the island disappeared, and even described the attempt made by a schoolmaster of Ardgour, Charles McClean, to set up a salvage operation some years later, 'thinking to find certain riches within the logh.' Glen Mor is more prone to earth tremors than anywhere else in the British Isles, and such tremors have been known to produce tidal waves in Loch Ness. Could this be a natural explanation for the disappearance of Ardgour Island? A severe earth tremor and a foam-crested tidal wave rearing up from the blackness of the loch could be suitably embroidered into an interesting legend. Modern investigators, notably in archaeology, are becoming more convinced that legends are based on fact, and that even the most unlikely tales are woven around a grain of truth.

A more recent story took place around the turn of the 20th century. A gypsy woman was trudging along a sandy path that ran alongside Loch Ness. She had been coming that way for years on her way from village to village selling her clothes pegs. Rounding a sudden bend she stopped dead in her tracks. There before her, basking in the bracken, lay a huge hideous monster. At the sight of the woman it swiftly slithered down the bank and disappeared into the waters of the loch. She had the impression of a long neck and tail and a heavy body. The whole thing happened too quickly to notice details, but she thought it was either black or dark grey in colour. Nothing would persuade her to use that path again, and from that day onwards she walked a long way out of her way over the hills rather than meet that hideous creature ever again.

Loch Ness is the largest body of freshwater in the British Isles, and the second deepest. It is 35 kilometres long, and over 1 kilometre wide in parts. Its greatest depth is about 225 metres. After dusk the Great Glen becomes an eerie place, and even the most phlegmatic visitor feels a vague sense of unease, an instinctive awareness of strange unseen things. It is certainly a fitting haunt for a monster. But until recent times, few people outside the Highlands had ever heard of the beastie.

Then, in July 1933, a company director and his wife had an alarming experience in the Great Glen. The Spicers were returning to London from a motoring holiday in Scotland. They had driven through Inverness and were on the road which runs beside the loch from Dores to Foyers. It was 4 o'clock on a clear and sunny afternoon. They saw what Mr Spicer described as a 'trunk-like thing' come out of the bracken. It crossed the road and disappeared into the loch. Mr Spicer said that the creature was 7 to 9 metres long and was the colour of an elephant.

One crisp, bright Sunday morning in November of the same year, Hugh Gray, an employee at the nearby British Aluminium Company plant, trudged up a sandy promontory covered by trees that overlooked Loch Ness. (At this point the loch is about 80 metres deep close to the shore.) The sun was shining, the air crystal clear – perfect conditions for taking photographs. Hugh Gray, a keen photographer, had already seen a creature of some kind in the loch and he hoped at some time to be able to take a picture of it. Reaching the top of the bluff he settled himself on a grassy bank with his camera beside him. Below, the River Foyers meandered through a patch of flat land, to empty its peat-stained waters into the loch, alongside the village of Lower Foyers. The loch itself was still and silent.

Later he told a newspaper reporter:

'I had hardly sat down when an object of considerable dimensions rose out of the loch 200 yards [180 metres] away. I immediately got my camera into position and snapped the object which was 2 or 3 feet [nearly 1 metre] above the surface of the water. I did not see any head, but there was a considerable motion from what I thought was a tail. I cannot give any definite opinion as to its size or appearance, except that it was of great size.'

When the national newspapers got hold of the story they gave it banner headlines on their front pages. Hugh Gray's photograph certainly hit the news. Claims of sightings flooded into the newspaper offices. All at once everyone was discussing the 'Loch Ness Monster', as one paper christened it. The other papers immediately followed suit and the name stuck.

People took sides for and against its existence, and the canny lochside dwellers, sensing a lucrative increase in tourism, did nothing to dispel the rumours of 'Nessy'. Hotels and pubs within the area were soon bulging with reporters, journalists and photographers, all eager to catch a glimpse of the fabulous monster.

Hugh Gray, a sensible man, submitted his photograph together with a written description, to Professor Graham Kerr, then Professor of Zoology at the University of Glasgow. The professor's reaction was immediate and categorical. He remarked:

'I see nothing in the photograph with a head like a seal nor do I see a body like an eel. Nor do I see two lateral fins such as have been described by the photographer. What I do see is a curved shape in the water with the appearance of vertical splashes rising from it. I find this picture which you have shown me utterly unconvincing as a photograph of any living thing.'

And, to make his position absolutely clear, Professor Kerr is supposed to have told reporters, 'It is absurd to suppose that a "monster" – as it is popularly conceived – can exist in Loch Ness. Absurd suggestions by untrained observers have been circulated recently.'

Hugh Gray's photograph of the monster.

Many searches for the monster have taken place including this one in a BBC programme.

Even to an 'untrained observer', the Gray photograph shows more than a curved shape in the water, and under a magnifying glass the two ball-like organs in the torso appear to be smooth, oval shaped and fleshy. Manchester University zoologists, although highly sceptical, finally said:

There appear to be two small black and white objects attached to the body, and while the one nearer the head might conceivably be the distinctive white-striped flipper of the lesser rorqual (a type of whale), the other object nearer the tail appears to be almost exactly similar but should certainly not be there if the creature were a lesser rorqual.'

It was beginning to seem that Professor Kerr may possibly have been a bit hasty in dismissing the Gray photograph. But if the monster was not a lesser rorqual, what was it?

After many other claimed sightings, the Loch Ness Monster allowed itself to be photographed for a second time. Mr R K Wilson, Fellow of the Royal College of Surgeons and a keen amateur naturalist and photographer, was motoring beside the loch early one April morning in 1934, with a camera and telephoto lens on the seat beside him. Pausing near Invermoriston, he noticed a flurry on the surface of the loch. There was the monster, its head and neck raised in the air, about 160 metres away. Snatching up his camera, Mr Wilson managed to expose two plates before the monster quietly submerged. Curiously, it did this by sinking vertically, as the second picture shows the head sliding beneath the waves.

Wilson was unbelievably lucky. The odds against being at exactly the right place at exactly the right time with a loaded camera, are enormous, as the people who did not believe in the Loch Ness Monster were quick to point out. This photograph showed what many witnesses had already described. A snake-like undulating neck, arching from a whale-like body to a small, pointed head. Again there is a suggestion of a bulbous organ growing from the top part of the creature's body. Unfortunately it is as tantalizingly vague as Hugh Gray's photograph. But many people were convinced that they were seeing an aquatic reptile, maybe of a species extinct for thousands of years. The controversy flared up again, but the official attitude remained unchanged – total disbelief.

Descriptions of the Loch Ness Monster since the first sighting have been very similar to each other. The size of the heavy, whale-like body ranges from between 6 to 9 metres, with four bulbous organs growing from it. Although there is some disagreement about the actual colour, everyone claims it has a small worm-like head on a long neck and also a long tail. However, these descriptions did not fit any of the known prehistoric reptiles – that is, until 1958. It was then that Francis Tully uncovered a fossil of a bizarre worm-like reptile, about 80 kilometres south of Chicago, USA, in Pennsylvanian (Upper Coal Age) deposits. It was later christened

Tullimonstrum. The creature was an invertebrate with a segmented body. It had a tiny head, a slender swan-like neck and a torpedo-shaped body ending in a powerful tail. It also had two bulbous organs growing on the fore part of its body. Chicago's Field Museum of Natural History believed it had lived in the sea or brackish water. This description is very like that of the creature seen in Loch Ness by numerous witnesses.

Since the 30s there have been endless other claims and sightings, a mounting mass of verbal evidence, difficult to dismiss out of hand. Witness after witness has come forward to testify to having seen the monster. Serious expeditions have been set up which have produced startling results and a number of films exist which claim to show the monster. One particular film, made in 1960, was shown to the Joint Air Reconnaissance Intelligence Centre of the Ministry of Defence, the foremost experts in analysing photographic images. They said that the thing shown on the film, '. . . . . leaves the conclusion that it probably is an animate object.'

In the face of mounting reports by reliable witnesses these theories of the scoffers appear a trifle thin: otter, waterfowl, vegetable matter filled with trapped gases, deer, boats seen in the distance, half-submerged trees, long grass snakes, peculiar waves, and even one suggestion that it could be a thresher shark swimming up from the Caledonian Canal. Warned of these possibilities is it likely that responsible investigators, engineers, school teachers, doctors and others would mistake vegetable matter or a long grass snake for the Loch Ness Monster?

Over recent years scientists have shown an increasing interest in the activities of the Loch Ness Monster, and their research has been both professional and thorough. The use of sonar equipment has produced some very interesting results but nothing finally conclusive. There is still some room for argument and disbelief. However, now that the Boston, USA-based Academy of Applied Science has started investigating there is every possibility that conclusive results will be obtained.

Already, sonar recordings show echoes from large moving objects, which scientists believe were not shoals of fish. There have also been a number of underwater colour photographs of

Research for the Loch Ness Monster has become more efficient with new equipment. The Academy of Applied Science in America have started investigating (above) and several underwater photographs such as this one (below right) have been taken. Other recent photographs such as this one taken by Anthony Shiels (below left) may be proof of a monster.

what appear to be huge swimming creatures. One experiment involving the use of sonar equipment, in conjunction with an underwater camera, produced startling results. A moving object was detected by the sonar, and fish echoes which appeared as small dots turned into streaks as the fish darted away from the object. The underwater camera, suspended at about 17 metres, took shots. The 16mm film was flown to the United States where it was developed and printed using the same computer-enhanced process used to clarify space photographs. One such photograph shows a paddle-like structure, believed to be a limb, about 2 or 3 metres long and over 1 metre wide, and behind that, what appears to be a second body with appendages. There is also a cine film which shows a large object moving away from the camera at approximately 15 kph.

A constant watch is now kept on the loch. Perhaps someday someone will come up with a clear, well-produced film that will wipe away all doubt about the Monster of Loch Ness.

An artist's impression of the monster.

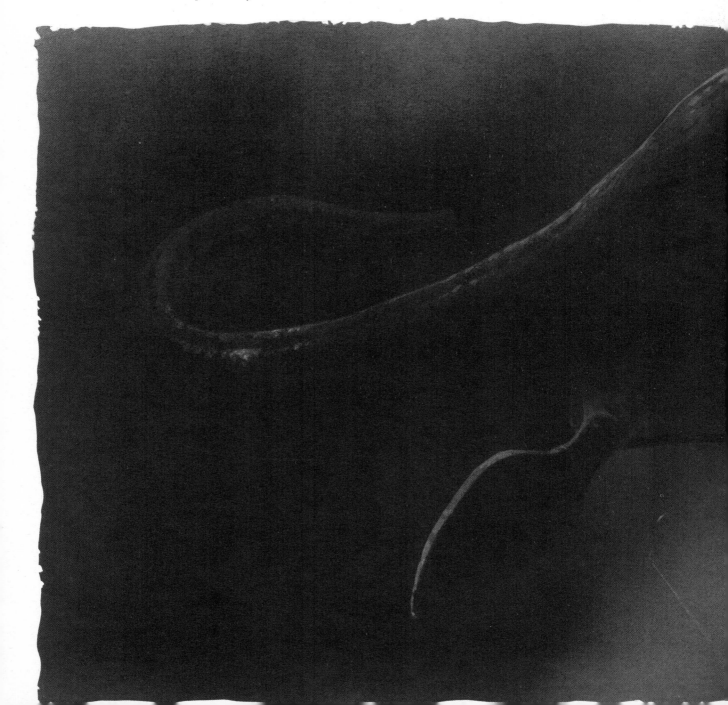

The Eighth Continent

He maintained that a large land mass once occupied most of the present North Atlantic Ocean.

'Land ahoy! Land ahoy!' The cheer went through the galley. They were home. The off-watch crew hurried to the prow of the ship. There, dead ahead, lay the metropolis shining in the early morning sun.

'Raise the beat,' shouted the captain.

The rowing master increased the rhythm that he was banging with his two wooden mallets. The trireme leaped forward, her battle ram scything through the Atlantic swell as the oarsmen increased their rate of rowing. They too would be glad to leave the dark, dank rowing decks for a spell ashore. It would be a merciful relief from the backbreaking monotony of the rowing benches.

A Greek statue of Poseidon, the god of the sea. 'The Ruler of the Sea' was the patron god of the early mariners who prayed to him for a safe voyage.

The trireme had passed the Pillars of Hercules some days ago and was on the last leg of the journey from Egypt with a cargo of spices, unguents and myrrh, fine Egyptian linen and curious jewels and scarabs. Hardened seamen though the crew were, they still disliked heading straight out into the 'True Ocean', the vast expanse of sea that surrounded their homeland.

It was a treacherous stretch of water that could suddenly turn into a raging inferno of huge spume-topped waves that smashed down on ships. Then oars were drawn in and sails furled, while the double-watch of steersmen fought to keep the prow of the galley pointed into the waves. Many a proud ship caught beam-on had capsized, going down with all hands. In times like that the crew could only pray that their god, Poseideon, Ruler of the Sea, would take pity and spare them.

The weather on this voyage had held good though, with blue skies and a hot sun shining down on the rollers coming at them from out of the west. Now they were under the steep cliffs heading for the entrance to the canal. The glare from the city was blinding in the mounting sun. On either side the walls of the canal rose steeply, topped by the houses and the trading quarter. Old friends shouted and waved to them. The canal was 90 metres wide and some said it was as much as 30 metres deep. In Greek measurements, it was certainly 50 stadia (about 9·5 kilometres) long. Gently they paddled on, nosing their way into the Great Harbour, a large ring of water crowded with shipping: ocean-going triremes, pot-bellied merchantmen capable of wallowing the length and breadth of the world, and smaller fishing vessels. In between the ships flashed skiffs and small boats. All day and night the harbour was bustling with activity.

Three great galleys were moving towards the canal entrance, line astern, obviously set for a long voyage. The leading captain cupped his hands and shouted, 'Crete'.

As the trireme crossed the Great Harbour, towards the underpass that would take them through to the second harbour, the crew could see the reason for the glare. The vast wall running down to the jetties was plated from top to bottom with a coating of bronze. A guard house dominated the entrance to the underpass.

The captain of the guard leaned over the wall and said, 'We didn't expect you for another month.'

'We had good weather and calm seas,' called back the captain of the trireme.

Carefully the steersman manoeuvred the galley into the brilliantly lit underpass, stone oil lamps and fire braziers lined the whole of the 3 stadia (about 550 metres) to the second harbour.

The underpass went under the major zone of land, the outer of two man-made rings built of solid rock. They were for recreation and sport. Pleasure gardens were planted with a wide variety of trees and plants, which were very high and beautiful owing to the richness of the soil. A wide race course ran the full circumference of the outer zone as the citizens were passionately fond of horse racing.

The returning trireme glided into the second harbour, which was less crowded than the first but equally noisy. This circular basin was not as wide as the first one, and the wall of its zone of land was plated with tin. Here there were underground docks given over to ship building and refitting. As they steered towards the next underpass the crew could see temples and great buildings nestling among the trees. Rowing through the underpass they arrived at the last of the circular basins, the inner harbour that surrounded the citadel.

The citadel stood before them, a shimmering mass of silver and gold. Quickly they made fast alongside the guard house, manned by the pick of the army, the king's trusted bodyguard. Passed by the officer of the guard, they hurried ashore, the captain anxious to report the success of his mission. The circular island citadel, centre of their world, was nearly one kilometre across. At the centre of the circular island stood the temple dedicated to Cleito and Poseidon, founders of the country. But the galley captain and his crew were making for Poseidon's own temple, to offer thanks for their safe return. The temple itself, 180 metres long and 90 metres wide, was covered in silver plate, its pinnacle in gold.

A vast golden statue of Poseidon in a chariot pulled by five winged horses stood at one end of the temple, the head of the god brushing the

roof. He was surrounded by 100 golden statues of water nymphs riding dolphins. Awed, the sailors honoured the god of the sea.

According to Plato, a Greek philosopher who lived in 4 BC, that world existed over 12 000 years ago. It was the metropolis of the lost continent of Atlantis. He began the legend of an island continent beyond the Pillars of Hercules (the two promontories on opposite sides of the east end of the Strait of Gibraltar). It was supposed to be the heart of a great and wonderful empire possessing a large population, golden-roofed cities, mighty armies and fleets of ships for invasion and conquest. In two of his books, Plato described Atlantis as an earthly paradise, a combination of mountain ranges, wide, deep rivers, fertile plains, rich mineral deposits, varied flora and fauna including elephants, and a thriving population.

He told how people of Atlantis and the neighbouring islands lived and were governed. How the 10 kings, the descendants of the union between the god, Poseidon, and the earthly woman, Cleito, met every five years or so to pass laws and govern the land. The ceremony

The sculptured head of a bull (above) and a fresco of dolphins (below), both from the Palace of Knossos, Crete. Could these have a connection with the lost city of Atlantis?

always began with a hunt. The kings were required to capture one of the bulls which ranged freely in the temple grounds and sacred groves. They could use staves and nooses but no weapons. When the bull was caught, it was sacrificed to the sea god, and its blood spilled across the column depicting the ancient laws.

The empire of Atlantis supposedly stretched from the Americas in the west (The True Continent) to parts of India, Egypt, The Black Sea, North Africa and coastal Spain and Portugal. Its people also probed northwards to Britain and the Baltic. Only the city state of Athens held out against Atlantis, actually carrying an army out into the Atlantic to invade the island. Plato

wrote the story as related to Solon, a Greek elder statesman, by the Egyptian priests when he made a visit to that country:

'Many great and wonderful deeds are recorded of your state [Athens] in our histories. But one of them exceeds all the rest in greatness and valour. For these histories tell of a mighty power which, unprovoked, made an expedition against the whole of Europe and Asia, and to which your city put an end. This power came forth out of the Atlantic Ocean, for in those days the Atlantic was navigable and there was an island situated in front of the straits which are called by you the Pillar of Herakles [Hercules]; this island was larger than Libya and Asia put together, and was the way to other islands, and from these you might pass to the whole of the opposite continent which surrounded the true ocean. . .

Now in this island of Atlantis there was a great and wonderful empire which had rule over the whole island and several others. This vast power, gathered into one, endeavoured to subdue at a blow our country and yours and the whole of the region within the straits; and then, Solon, your country shone forth, in the excellence of her virtue and strength, among all mankind. She was pre-eminent in courage and military skill, and was the leader of the Hellenes. And when the rest fell off from her, being compelled to stand alone, after having undergone the very extremity of dangers, she defeated and triumphed over the invaders, and preserved from slavery

145

those who were not yet subjugated, and generously liberated all the rest of us who dwelt within the pillars. But afterwards there occurred violent earthquakes and floods; and in a single day and night of misfortune all your warlike men in a body sank into the earth, and the island of Atlantis in like manner disappeared into the depths of the sea. For which reason the sea in those parts is impenetrable, because there is a shoal of mud in the way; and this was caused by the subsidence of the island.'

Atlantis is one of the world's greatest mysteries. Ever since Plato first published his story, people have been both attracted and puzzled by it. Some have explained it away as an extremely imaginative fairy story; others have justified the truth of it by establishing the exact position of the island and locating remnants of it.

Aristotle, another Greek philosopher and pupil of Plato, compared the story of Atlantis with some of the poetic fiction of the Greek poet, Homer, used to help out a narrative. He suggested that Plato sank his Atlantis in the depths of the ocean to forestall anyone who might ask for the true location of the island. As he unkindly put it: 'The man who dreamed it up made it vanish.'

This has been the stand of Plato's opponents down the centuries, but Plato had, and still has, his share of champions. The lost continent has been sought by scholars as far afield as the Atlantic, North and South America, North Africa, The Holy Land, the Sahara desert, the Crimea and Southern Russia, Belgium and the Netherlands, and more recently, the islands of Crete and Thera. These scholars have sought evidence on the sea bed of the Atlantic, seeking to establish a land bridge, and in the art and culture of the Incas of Peru and the people of the Canary Islands.

Until modern times, the search for Atlantis has usually been followed outside the Mediterranean, beyond the Pillars of Hercules, and many physical points of similarity have been suggested between Plato's account and existing islands. Plato mentions black, white and red rocks, and volcanic rocks in these colours are found in the Canaries, the Azores and other Atlantic islands. He also refers to hot and cold springs. The springs, like the coloured rocks, still exist in the Azores.

Aristotle and Plato from a detail of a fresco in the Vatican Palace, by Raphael.

When the Spaniards discovered the Canary Islands in the 14th century, the islanders, once the Europeans could communicate with them, expressed surprise that other people were still alive. According to their legends all humanity perished in a catastrophe, when the land sank into the sea, but that some mountains, their present home, remained above water. The islanders displayed many of the customs described by Plato, in an odd mixture of civilized culture and Stone Age barbarism. Among other things they had a selective monarchy of 10 kings; they worshipped the Sun; they mummified their dead; they built houses of closely fitting stones with walls coloured red, white and black, and great circular fortifications; they used a system of canal irrigation; they made pottery similar to the American Indians; they possessed literature and poetry, and had a written alphabetical language. Many of these practices agree closely with Plato's account of Atlantis.

A book published in America in 1882, *Atlantis, the Antediluvian World* by Ignatius Donnelly, did much to revive interest in Plato's island. A true believer, Donnelly set out to show that Atlantis had been a link between the Old World and the New, and supported this with a list of 13 propositions. Following Plato, he began by placing Atlantis opposite the mouth of the Mediterranean. He said that the great island was the cradle of Sun worship, the source of bronze and iron working, the forerunner of the Phoenician alphabet. Its people colonized Egypt, spread through the Mediterranean, Black Sea and Caspian Sea, and reached Britain and the Baltic. It was the original 'Garden of Eden'. He attempted to show a similarity between Egyptian hieroglyphics and the Mayan alphabet, and a likeness between pottery east and west of the Atlantic. There are many other similarities which have been discovered over the years. The calendar of the Mayans had 18 months of 20 days, as did the calendar of the ancient Egyptians. The Egyptians constructed great pyramids, as did the ancients of Central and South America. Although Donnelly's book is scorned by serious scholars and scientists, in its day it made a tremendous impact. Gladstone, the British prime minister of the time, attempted to set up an expedition to seek out the sunken city, but his cabinet dissuaded him from the venture.

On the island of Lanzaroti in the Canaries, twigs can be ignited by the heat of volcanic action.

One of Donnelly's best-known disciples, Lewis Spence, tried to put Donnelly's original views on a firm scientific footing. He maintained that a large land mass once occupied most of the present North Atlantic Ocean. This, he argues, first broke down into two island continents, Atlantis and Antilla. Atlantis was not far west of Spain, and Antilla near the present West Indies. Atlantis finally submerged about 10 000 BC; Antilla still exists in part in the West Indian archipelago. His moderate views appear to be quite plausible. There is undoubtedly a mid-Atlantic ridge running from the South Atlantic to Iceland, lying at an average depth of about 1·5 kilometres below the surface. It actually comes to the surface in a few places: the Azores, Ascension Island and Tristan da Cunha.

The ancients of Central and South America constructed great pyramids.

The British prime minister, W E Gladstone, who wanted to mount an expedition to Atlantis.

Is this a land mass that sunk at some time? Modern scientists and oceanographers reject the idea of an Atlantic ridge being the remnant of a sunken continent. They believe that the ridge is the result of volcanic activity which raised it from the floor of the ocean. Modern scholars turn their eyes in other directions in search of Atlantis. The very name has been misleading. 'Atlantis' is not derived from 'Atlantic', but means 'Island of Atlas'. Atlas is the mythical Greek hero who held the world on his shoulders. The place where he was supposed to have stood may have been well inside the Mediterranean, before the Greeks placed him on the Atlas mountain range of Morocco.

Some scholars have thought that Atlantis was in Nigeria. J Spanuth, however, in his book, *Atlantis, the Mystery Unravelled*, published in 1956, claims to have seen the walls of the celebrated citadel below the waters off Heligoland, an island in the North Sea. Other theories on Atlantis that have been put forward, suggest that a number of ancient cultures that are defin-

itely known to have existed, could each, according to the particular researcher, have been the lost continent.

A favourite among the possibilities is a place called Tartessos, or Tarshish as the Greeks called it. It is thought to have been a great and prosperous civilization, located somewhere on the Atlantic coast of Spain, rich in mineral wealth. Tartessos was reputed to have records going back 6000 years, and the Rio Tinto copper mines, lying roughly in the supposed area of the city-state, are estimated to be 8000 to 10 000 years old. There are references to Tartessos in the ancient writings of the Hebrews, Greeks, Assyrians and Romans. The Bible tells of Tarshish ships and voyages to Tarshish.

Tartessos itself has never been discovered, although large building blocks have been found and Mrs E M Wilshaw, author of *Atlantis in Andalusia*, who has studied the area for 25 years, believes that Tartessos may be buried beneath the present day city of Seville. But she believes that Tartessos was a colony of Atlantis.

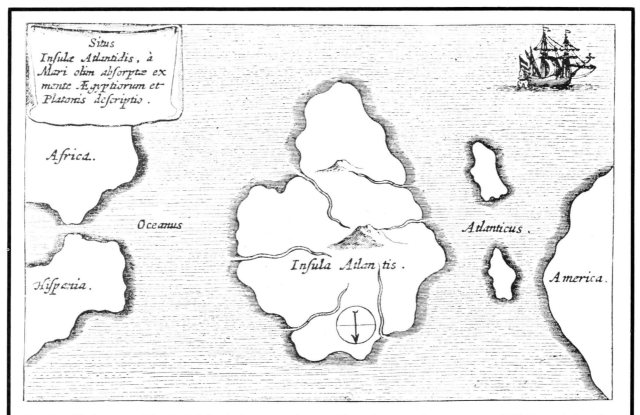

In this old chart, the island of Atlantis has been placed midway between the continents of Africa and America. The chart has been drawn upside down to us, before the introduction of north and south.

150

Some recent theories place Atlantis in Minoan Crete and/or the island of Thera in the eastern Mediterranean. The idea was first put forward as a possible solution in 1909 by K T Frost. He wrote:

'The whole description of Atlantis which is given in the *Timaeus* and the *Critias* has features so thoroughly Minoan that even Plato could not have invented so many unsuspected facts. The Great Harbour, for example, with its shipping and its merchants coming from all parts, the elaborate bathrooms, the stadium, and the solemn sacrifice of a bull are all thoroughly, though not exclusively, Minoan; but when we read how the bull is hunted "in the temple of Poseidon without weapons but with staves and nooses", we have an unmistakable description of the bull-ring at Knossos (the king's palace) the very thing which struck foreigners most and which gave rise to the legend of the Minotaur.'

Frost's case has been subsequently strengthened by Professor Marmatos, of the Greek Archaeological Service, who has demonstrated that the sudden disappearance of the Minoan empire was due to a natural catastrophe of great violence and destructive power – a volcanic eruption sometime between 1500 and 1470 BC.

The bull-ring at Knossos gave rise to the legend of the Minotaur.

This echoes Plato's words:

'But afterwards there occurred violent earthquakes and floods, and in a single day and night of misfortune the island of Atlantis disappeared in the depths of the sea.'

But perhaps after all the 'Atlantic' champions may have the last word. Edgar Cayce, an American psychic researcher and ESP (Extra-sensory perception) investigator, has previously given, between 1923 and 1944, many psychic 'readings' about life in Atlantis. He claimed that the lost continent lay off the Bahamas, and then went on to make an extraordinary statement: 'Poseida will be among the first portions of Atlantis to rise again. Expected in '68 and '69. Not so far away.'

The underwater search for Atlantis continues.
Photographs are used to build up a wide picture.

Incredible as it may seem, several buildings seem to be coming to the surface off Bimini and Andros. No one has yet established what they are or how old they are, but the appearance of these mysterious buildings is taking place at exactly the spot predicted by Cayce in 1940!

To further confuse the situation, a Frenchman, Jean Albert Foëx, has produced an explanation, both simple and practical. It is not based on cultural ideas or myths and legend, but on accepted scientific fact. There is general agreement among geologists and oceanographers, that while the rise of the level of the sea over the last several thousand years has been about 30 centimetres per century, there was a much more rapid rise at a time before that. Around the 10th century BC, the level of the sea rose 130 to 150 metres, due to the floods released by the melting glaciers of the last Ice Age. These were accompanied by rains and volcanic eruptions, especially in the volcanic zones of the Atlantic.

By projecting the Atlantic islands as they then were, dropping the water by 150 metres, it shows that the present islands as well as the coasts of America, Spain, Portugal and North Africa were far greater land masses, certainly capable of supporting an advanced civilization. A drop in the sea of 150 metres would also reveal many more islands than now exist. Even the time element is consistent. Plato places the sinking of Atlantis, as reported by the Egyptian priests, as 11 250 years ago. Modern science gives 10 000 BC as the end of the last European glaciers.

Could Plato have been right, or is the legend of Atlantis a rather nice fairytale?

The photographs are carefully selected and placed together to make up a jigsaw picture of the area that might have been Atlantis.

153

Postscript

There are more things in heaven and earth, Horatio,
Than are dreamt of in your philosophy.

Shakespeare *Hamlet* Act I scene V

Index